The History We Carry

A Daughter's Memoir

Margaret Whitford

SHE WRITES PRESS

Published in 2026 by
She Writes Press, an imprint of The Stable Book Group

1569 Solano Ave #546
Berkeley, CA 94707
https://shewritespress.com
Library of Congress Control Number: 2026904363
ISBN: 979-8-89636-322-4
eISBN: 979-8-89636-323-1

Interior Designer: Tabitha Lahr

Printed in the United States

Names and identifying characteristics have been changed to protect the privacy of certain individuals.

For, and in memory of, my mother
Margaret Radzin Lehr

Born February 7, 1923, in Riga, Latvia
Died February 20, 2012, in Concord, Massachusetts

Contents

Author's Note

As with most memoirs, this book is shaped by memory. My recollections may differ from those of others who shared the same moments. I have endeavored to remain faithful to the truth of my experience.

Over the years, my mother spoke occasionally about the Second World War and other aspects of her life. I preserved many of her stories through recorded interviews and detailed note-taking. In bringing her to life on the page, I have drawn on her personal accounts, supplemented by my own research into the war and the enduring effects of complex trauma.

When writing about my mother as a young woman in Latvia and Austria—years that unfolded before I was born—I have generally chosen to refer to her by her Latvian name, Margrieta. In doing so, I hope to honor her as an individual whose identity extended beyond motherhood.

In some instances, I have changed names, characteristics, and identifying details to protect the privacy of those involved. Some dialogue has been recreated.

A World of Two

I picture my mother lying on her hospital bed, the same one she has occupied for the last twelve days. The space is in shadow, the only light coming from the hallway. The room smells empty. No flowers or scented candles—she wouldn't have wanted those. The sound of retreating footfalls in the corridor or a muffled voice from another part of the hospital occasionally interrupts the silence. Her breathing is shallow, until the moment it stops altogether. It happens so quietly, no one notices at first.

When my mother died in Concord, I was an ocean away, in a Paris hotel. Another day had already started. That remove feels familiar—geography and time following an established pattern.

In the morning's early hours, I lay next to my husband, Tom, on a king-sized bed in a room of marble-inlaid tables and still-life paintings in gilded frames, the walls covered in red-and-gold-striped paper. I heard only the sounds of the night, a faint breeze moving through the magnolia trees in the courtyard and an occasional car gliding along the boulevard.

While Tom slept, I lay awake, thinking about my mother. I had started to understand that we wouldn't make it back in time. My mother would either be dead or so unresponsive that there could be no last words between us.

Tom read my brother Billy's email while I was taking a shower. I knew from the way he walked into the bathroom, but he still had to say the words: "Your mother is dead." *Years from now*, I thought, *I will be able to replay this moment in my mind*. He stood there, naked, looking both vulnerable and strong, his hand on the shower wall ready to reach for me.

My brothers and sister wanted to touch our mother after she died because she had not welcomed that while living. She would allow a hug or a kiss in greeting or farewell but shrugged you off if you lingered in the embrace.

Henry would have stroked her sparse hair, cut short after she could no longer shape it into a twist. He might have teased her about finally being able to touch her hair, something she loathed. Lydia might have rubbed her feet, those odd feet, with such high arches her toes curled to reach the ground. Her feet shaped by childhood polio and old age, missing the little toe on one foot, removed because of frostbite suffered during the Second World War. She could never find comfortable shoes, so she wore Birkenstock sandals year-round, donning socks with them in winter.

Billy would have rested his hand on her shoulder, let his fingers travel the length of her arm. He might have held her hand, bent at strange angles by arthritis and with the bones loose under the skin. Had I been there, I would also have been drawn to her hands, so small that they reminded me of a child's. She kept her nails short and immaculate, a habit she'd adopted in medical school, and one I try to emulate. I might have traced the line of her aquiline nose and the contour of her jaw, fondled her cheek and pressed my fingers to her high cheekbones, a sign of her Slavic heritage, she once told me.

Her sandals and the pair of socks she last wore with them are mine now, safeguarded in a box in the back of my closet. Those Birkenstocks, the insoles shaped over time by the pressure of her feet, her navy-blue socks. I wanted the last of her clothing, something that had touched her. I run my hands over the smooth cork, hold the socks to my cheek, the much-washed cotton soft. I thought the socks might retain the cool, dry scent of her.

Our plane to Massachusetts departed in the afternoon, so Tom and I filled the morning with small errands—the purchase of a journal of good paper with a red ribbon to mark my place—and one last view of Notre-Dame. Each gesture, every step I made, accompanied by a voice in my head repeating, *Your mother is dead.*

The air smelled of diesel fuel and wet earth. My left arm entwined with Tom's right, I rested my hand on his steady forearm, eavesdropped on the conversations around me, catching only phrases. I thought how these strangers knew nothing of my grief and I nothing of theirs. A rare winter's morning, fresh with rain-washed skies, and sunlight bathing the bone-colored stone of centuries-old buildings. I noticed the quality of the light, its unusual clarity. Tom and I had introduced my mother to Paris on a trip years before. *She will never see it again*, I thought, trying to absorb its beauty on her behalf.

I saw my mother for the last time three months before she died, at Thanksgiving. The holiday had been one of her favorites—no religious overtones, just a festive gathering of family and friends. She enjoyed turkey but never had it unless someone else cooked it for her. She savored Billy's black-eyed peas sautéed with onion, garlic, and parsley, seasoned with curry or cumin. When I was a child and we still celebrated Thanksgiving as a family, my mother always made black-eyed peas for my Southern father, but her version was bland, just boiled peas with bacon, salt, and pepper. She never liked the dish until my brother introduced his version.

While conversation swirled, she sat quietly at the island in my brother's kitchen. The scent of turkey roasting filled the room. Hands reached around her to spread soft Brie cheese on a cracker, fork a piece of smoked salmon, scoop up spiced pecans, but she took no part. The surrender of her shoulders, the way she leaned forward and stared without focus made her seem unreachable. It struck me then that we wouldn't share another Thanksgiving.

Two days later, I stopped by her apartment to say goodbye. She'd left the door unlocked to avoid having to rise to open it, so I tapped lightly and stepped into her living room. She sat in a recliner in front of her never-used terrace, surrounded by books she no longer read. Her wheeled walker with its built-in seat stood next to her chair. She wore a dark T-shirt and leggings, baggy on her thin thighs. Her skin, now always without makeup, looked sallow.

I molded my face into a smile, understanding that whatever energy existed in that room would have to come from me. But my expression wasn't sufficient to engage her, so I didn't linger. I hugged her, careful not to hold on tightly for fear of causing her pain. Osteoporosis and arthritis had weakened her neck and back. She raised her arms to rest her hands on my shoulders as I kissed her cheek, and then dropped them, their weight too much to bear.

When I reached the hallway, I turned back to hug her once more. I sensed I might not get another chance. Given her frailty, she could die suddenly without any time to prepare, though that's not what I believed would happen. Her health problems were chronic, not acute. If she believed her death imminent, she would ask for me. I was sure of it. Her call would have come in the morning when her breathing was better and her voice stronger. "Margaret," she would have said, "will you come to see me?" And I would have gone.

A family friend, who as a young boy had found in my mother the mother he had wanted, told me of one small regret. He used the word "small," and I thought, *How lucky to be able to describe regret in that way*. In January, about a month before my mother died, she had asked him to visit. "I wish I'd gone," he said, "but I couldn't get away at the time."

Instead of asking me to visit, she asked for my writing: "Send me your essays." I picked several, two of which featured her. She called later to compliment me on the briefest piece, an interpretation of a photograph my father had taken of her decades before. "You captured us," she said.

Her only question about the work I'd sent related to the death of Tom's and my dog. "How did Annie die?" I told her of the clear September day, the warmth of the sun, the grass on which we had laid a blanket for Annie, our vet who had suggested we have our little terrier die in the park. I described how I'd petted Annie, my caress the last thing she felt. I told her that I'd recognized the moment Annie died by the way the skin around her skull slackened suddenly beneath my hand. Or perhaps I didn't tell her this story. Perhaps I only wish now that I had. Perhaps instead I told her how Annie couldn't eat toward the end, that Tom and I couldn't bear her struggle. That some light had gone from her eyes and so we knew it was time. Perhaps this is what my mother wanted to know.

The words of one of those essays haunt me and I wish I had not sent it, even though my mother had read earlier drafts of the same piece. I dwell on how she might have read the last line: "I love my mother and believe she loves me. Intimacy and love are not the same thing, though, however much I wish they were." Did she conclude in the weeks before she died that we'd already said all we had to say to each other? Or had she determined that we could not overcome what separated us, and so decided not to spend her waning strength trying?

Sometimes I think my mother died of decisiveness, though I may be investing her with more agency than is justified. Nevertheless, it seems to me now that she directed her final days, becoming the author of her own ending.

Two weeks before she died, she dislocated her right shoulder reaching to put away a can of soup. Not a life-threatening incident; rather, it proved to be an opportunistic injury. The consulting orthopedic surgeon confirmed what she already knew—a shoulder replacement wasn't an option. Physical therapy was her only choice, but it couldn't restore her shoulder. At best, she might have regained use of her hand, wrist, and elbow.

She had lost ten pounds in the two months before her injury. Maybe she had hoped to hasten her death by depleting whatever physical strength she still possessed. Once hospitalized, she resisted eating and refused all food during her last couple of days, accelerating her decline.

She told others that she wanted to die, that she didn't want to live past eighty-nine, the same age at which her mother had died. And in more subtle ways she had been withdrawing from those who loved her, refusing invitations for lunch or a visit to a museum. Billy's offers to linger with her after their weekly trip to the grocery store were gently rebuffed. "No, darling," she would say. "You're so busy. You can go."

Billy has suggested that she was trying to prepare us for her death, fading away gradually so that we could grow accustomed to her absence. He understands her behavior as protective of us, but I think it had more to do with her desire to depart.

Once, when I asked her to tell me about her prayers, she said, "I pray that I will be able to wash my hair in the shower." A prayer not to fall, to be able to raise her arms up to lather her hair and rinse the soap away. Perhaps she decided then she would not endure much longer.

In the first week of her hospitalization, she agreed to physical therapy, but once she understood that she could enter hospice while remaining in the same facility—the same bed, in fact—she abandoned rehabilitation and set her will to dying.

I have reread the emails Billy sent after my mother's injury, so that some passages are seared in my memory. The list of recipients grew longer over time, as my brother sought to enlarge the circle to include all those who nurtured some claim on my mother. His daily missives detailed my mother's injury, treatment, and prognosis; then her decision to enter hospice; and, finally, her death.

I retrieve my journal from that time, its cover smooth and hard, like judgment. I scan the pages searching for what preoccupied me during those days, looking for reasons I didn't go to Concord—a two-day board meeting in Pittsburgh, meetings in Philadelphia to oversee renovations to our new home, a long-anticipated trip to France with commitments to honor there. I am obsessive in my review, as if within these pages I will find an explanation for why I was not with my mother when she died.

I reasoned that others were rallying around her. Billy's mother-in-law would deliver the "right yogurt," the only one my mother said she would eat. Tom's sister Barbara would visit with her French bulldog, entertaining my mother with his antics. Billy and his wife would advocate on her behalf, ensuring she received expert and responsive care.

And I didn't think her accident would lead so quickly to her death, nor did anyone else. I thought her injury might accelerate a physical decline, but I told myself my mother and I still had time.

I felt relief at being elsewhere. *Thank God*, I thought. *This is not my responsibility.*

My mother reinforced my decision to delay going to her, though I doubt she considered how I would interpret her behavior. She didn't have a phone in her room and insisted she didn't want one. During one of Barbara's early visits, she offered to call me on her cell phone so that my mother could speak with me. My mother refused, saying she was too tired to talk on the phone, and then regaled Barbara with stories for the next two hours.

Barbara had wanted to reassure me about my mother's condition and to express admiration for her skills as a storyteller, but that's not what I heard in her account. I heard only that my mother had rejected the chance to speak to me.

My mother made the decision to enter hospice on the Friday that Tom and I arrived in Paris. We spent the morning rearranging our schedule. I'm not sure how quickly we could have returned to Massachusetts if we had canceled all of our plans to take the next available flight. I wanted to stay for the weekend to visit friends in Provence who were expecting us, before returning to Paris for the flight to Boston. I thought of the visit as storing up happiness for what was to come.

My sister and brothers spent my mother's last lucid day with her, Lydia and Henry having driven to Concord that same Sunday. For much of the time, she refused pain medication so she could remain clearheaded. Later, her pain escalated, requiring hours to bring it under control. No doubt that choice weakened her further.

Family friends visited. Some lingered with her and tried to make her laugh—a story about a beloved dog or cat, even a turtle, would have done the trick. She said sometimes that she preferred animals to people. I understand what she meant; I've felt the same way. Animals never disappointed her. They never disappointed me.

She spoke with others by phone or asked that final messages be conveyed on her behalf. Never one to equivocate, she began those conversations with, "I am going to die."

"You could talk to her about anything," Billy told me.

I have a few photographs taken of her that last weekend. In one, my mother's face dominates the frame. She rests her head on a large pillow and looks toward someone in the room, not the person holding the camera. The light makes me believe it might have been sunny outside. Where her pale blue cotton gown has slipped, the top of her bare right shoulder is visible, the skin remarkably smooth. I look for the black strap from her underwire bra, surprised she was willing to part with it. Eyes alight, she smiles with her mouth open, as if she is about to or has just stopped laughing.

She assured my brothers and sister that she would be around. She would come to them in dreams, or in some other form. Once, long ago, she told me a story about her paternal grandmother's death, a tale she repeated before she died. Her father dreamed his mother was calling to him, but he could not respond. He learned the next day that she had died during the night. All of the clocks in his house had stopped at the moment of her death.

My mother didn't believe in heaven in any conventional sense. She envisioned each of us as an infinitesimal part of an incomprehensible whole, points of energy that endured after the body died so that a person was never truly lost, merely returned to the beginning.

If I'd been with her, I might have revisited the questions I'd asked about heaven as a child. *Will I know I am there? Will we recognize each other?* I would have tried to make her smile, so I would have asked her to find Gilbert and Annie, Tom's and my Jack Russell terriers. *Make sure they are getting along with Bruce*, our family's German shepherd, and the dog my mother loved above all others.

It surprised me that during her final days she talked about recipes, wanting to convey the essentials for two of her standards: Hungarian goulash and chicken in sour cream and white wine. For the former, she didn't provide any instructions, only insisted we use authentic Hungarian paprika, the hot stuff.

Years ago, she almost poisoned our father's medical residents at a dinner party ("poison" being our father's choice of words) by serving over-spiced goulash. An impatient and often reluctant cook, she hadn't tasted it. In fact, she rarely ate the finished dish, relying instead on her staples—kielbasa and sauerkraut, Spam and brown Swedish crackers, pearl-barley porridge loaded with sour cream and butter. Sometimes I wondered if these dishes reminded her of her native Latvia, especially during the war, when such food would have been a godsend.

For her chicken in sour cream recipe, one of my favorite dishes as a child, she provided a little more information: "Simmer whole chicken breasts stuffed with parsley in butter and white wine. When done, tear the chicken off the bone under running water while still hot, because if you wait until cold you cannot do it. Add more wine and sour cream. Two big glasses of wine."

The lack of precision around quantities is typical. When my sister, by then cooking on her own, once asked how much garlic to put in tomato sauce, our mother told her to mince garlic until her hands tired. Lydia, a sculptor, had strong hands, so the advice yielded unintended consequences.

My mother never wanted company in the kitchen. Once when I was seven or eight, I wandered in, drawn by the scent of butter and onions, hopeful she might teach me something about cooking. She stood by the stove, a spatula in her right hand, concentrating on stirring whatever resided in the large iron and enamel Dutch oven she favored. "Mom, can I help?" I asked. "Look," she said. "Either I do it, or you do it." I remember thinking, *But I'm just a kid, and I can't do this if you won't help me.*

The day before she died, she passed on her recipes, as if to encourage us to discover ways to nourish ourselves.

My mother also recalled music important to her, in particular a song from the Second World War, "Lili Marleen," popular ultimately with both German and American troops. Originally sung by Lale Andersen, Marlene Dietrich covered it later. From her hospital bed, my mother sang the song in the original German and then translated the lyrics into English, while insisting the German version was better.

Her singing, it seems to me, was part of a performance, a finale meant to leave her audience enthralled. She could rise to the occasion when she chose, especially if it offered her an opportunity to exceed people's expectations. She did so in the immediate aftermath of my father's death, when many anticipated she would be incapable of coping, and she would also do so in the circumstances of her own.

The song's first stanza, describing a sentry who waits and longs for his love and the private world they inhabit, stays with me. I find myself wondering with whom my mother identified—the sentry or his love. I am inclined to believe she cast herself as Lili Marleen, for I see myself so clearly as the soldier. I waited—for our world of two, for an unrestrained closeness to my mother. I waited for her to reach for me. She didn't. But I didn't reach for her either, and so I am complicit in my own pain.

We arrived in Concord less than twenty-four hours after my mother had died. Night had fallen by the time we reached Billy's house. I walked into the kitchen, the room bathed in soft light, the space warm. I hugged my brothers and sister, struck by how easily my body molded to each of theirs. I saw fatigue in their faces—it mirrored my own—and something else I couldn't identify. I think now it might have been relief. The vigil had ended, successfully concluded in what my brother Henry characterized as a "good death." I am alone in thinking otherwise, but I understand what he meant. My mother had wanted to die and managed to do so with grace. Just not a grace that included me.

The next day, I composed her obituary at the island in Billy's kitchen, a brief entry for the local paper. She had been adamant about not wanting a funeral, suggesting we give a party in her honor instead. I wrote, "A celebration of her life will be scheduled for this spring," the timing a guess.

In lieu of the flowers she never appreciated, discouraging us from sending bouquets, even on Mother's Day, I suggested donations to the Humane Society. When we emptied her apartment, I collected the small stuffed bears the organization had sent her in recognition of her generosity. One of them wears a heart-shaped pendant identifying him as "Margaret's Bear." I see some irony in my reaching for her stuffed animals, her metal Disney cartoon figurines—toys, essentially—when I can't remember us ever sharing any playful moments.

That little bear rests among my other stuffed animals on an uppermost shelf in my office, a space I gave to them rather than to books. I still have the now threadbare black-and-white cocker spaniel I cherished as a child, a toy I'd named Cookie. Aside from a brief fascination with Barbie dolls, I always preferred stuffed animals. Sometimes I view my preference as predictive of my adult life without the child Tom and I hoped for, that absence relieved by the presence of Gilbert and Annie.

My favorite toy as a very young child was a stuffed gorilla, a companion I brought everywhere, though I have only the vaguest recollection of him. About four years old, I stand in the sunshine in our backyard, holding the gorilla tightly to my chest. He eventually disintegrated to such a dismal condition that my mother threw him away one night while I slept, believing the toy had become a hazard. Decades later she sent me another stuffed gorilla, wrapped in tissue paper with a note that said only "Love, Mom." He sits next to a stuffed wolf I gave her long ago and reclaimed after her death. I bought the toy on impulse and then felt ridiculous, but she was delighted. She kept him next to her on her living room sofa.

And since some description of her death, other than date and location, seemed necessary for the obituary, I wrote, "Surrounded by her family, Margaret died as she lived, with beauty and courage." I kept it simple, if not entirely accurate. Because I was not with her when she died, implying otherwise serves as a reminder.

"Margaret has my history," my mother told my sister-in-law not long before she died. She would have been referring to the interviews I'd conducted during the last decade of her life—fifteen in all, clustered at the beginning and end of those years, the final one not even an interview, only my notes for a discussion we didn't have, because by then she had lost patience with my questions.

The idea of interviewing her occurred to me on an airplane, one of the few things I remember about that trip. Tom sat next to me, our first-class seats possible because of all the miles he'd accumulated traveling for his employer. Our destination not important during that suspended time between departure and arrival. My head against the window, I studied cloud formations, and below them, a landscape of geometric shapes in taupe and green, the gray threads of road. The hum of the plane's engines steady at that altitude, a white noise easy to ignore. The window cool against my temple, the upholstered seat soothing where it cradled my spine.

My thoughts traveled to my mother, who lived then in Texas's Hill Country, some fifteen hundred miles from my home in Pennsylvania. The act of travel may have prompted me to think of her, for I see now, I was always in motion where she was concerned, either moving away or trying to find my way back.

After my mother died, my siblings and I divided up her furniture and books, her clothing, whatever meant something to one or all of us. We behaved well, encouraging each other to choose what we each wanted without any competition. I took her cotton sarongs, because they reminded me of one of my last visits to Texas. I had opened the drawer of a carved mahogany chest in her living room and found the colorful pieces of fabric, some with fanciful designs of flowers, others with fish.

"What are these?" I asked my mother. "They're pretty."

"Oh, I bought them in Concord. They're sarongs, I wore them in Maine." By then it had been several years since she'd visited Billy and his family at their summer home.

"I'll give them to you," she offered.

"That would be very nice. I've been looking for something to wear over a bathing suit."

She showed me how to tie them around my hips. I noticed she hesitated over some pieces and then returned them to the drawer. I wondered, but did not ask, when she intended to wear them. Still, I liked the idea that she could see their future use. She sometimes wore them as skirts, she said. I imagined her navigating conservative Fredericksburg attired in a black T-shirt and a colorful length of cloth, Birkenstocks on her feet. I wondered at the impression she made, even as I recognized she wouldn't have cared.

From her apartment, I also took one of the three wedding bands she wore, the ring always a little large for her finger. I added it to the two wedding bands I wear, one from my wedding day and the second from Tom's and my first anniversary. It comforts me to worry the rose-yellow band as she once did, twisting it around my finger.

My brothers and sister agreed that our mother's boxes of photographs, albums, an old, battered suitcase—one I will be unable to open for months—should go to me, the oldest child. They accepted my designation as her historian. I wonder if they recognized what I see. The historian's role requires distance.

Displacement

As long as my mother lived, I could put off a reckoning, a coming to terms with the mystery of us. I didn't have to examine the distance between my mother and me because I told myself it was temporary—long-lasting, but not permanent.

For months after she died, I did little with the interviews, photographs, and other memorabilia that had come into my keeping. I kept her old suitcase where I could see it, but unopened. At the same time, I knew my mother's past waited for me. Her history is also my history, including the years before I was born.

When I do return to the interviews, the majority of which I taped, I do so initially to hear her voice again, her Latvian accent like the taste of mulled wine. As soon as she started to speak, it was clear she was from somewhere else. She drew out the sounds of vowels as if they could be tasted. *Darling* became *daahling* and my brother Billy's name, *Beely*. Though her command of English was excellent, her vocabulary could be off the mark. She once complimented my husband Tom for his *billboard abs* and me for what she viewed as my strength and dependability by telling me I was a *brick*.

My discussions with my mother extended beyond her wartime experiences, but when she spoke of the history bequeathed to me, I think she meant those memories. I'd grown up with her stories of the Second World War, especially those that privileged drama over deprivation. I understood she had survived threats so many others had not, and in that sense, had triumphed. But I did not consider the cost of that victory.

My mother once observed that small countries like her native Latvia often possess a nuanced understanding of world events. They do not make history. They adapt to survive.

Latvia was occupied three times during the war, starting with the Russian invasion in June 1940. On August 5, the country was incorporated into the Soviet Union as its fifteenth republic, ending twenty years of independence. The NKVD—the "politicos," my mother called them—quickly transformed public and private life.

Freedoms, once assured, disappear. My grandparents, Lee and Paul, surrender their radio, and with it, access to the outside world. Soviet-sanctioned publications replace the various newspapers that used to accumulate on Paul's desk. Loudspeakers, like cancerous tumors, distort the facades of Riga's art nouveau buildings, so that a city familiar to my mother since childhood grows alien. Incessant broadcasts, alternating between praise of Soviet achievements and patriotic music, shatter the capital's calm.

"Schoolchildren were led out onto the streets. We were forced to go in marches down the streets and hail the Russian Army. Literally," my mother said. I picture my mother, Margrieta, seventeen that summer and anticipating her final year in the gymnasium, the girls' secondary school preparing her for university. Soviet flags and placards bearing Stalin's image surround her, his likeness modified to camouflage his smallpox-scarred skin. His dazzling smile never reaches the black emptiness of his eyes. The too-loud music, meant to be stirring, sounds like a lament. Margrieta looks at the red flag with the gold hammer and sickle, the color raw against the blue sky, and wants to scream that it's not her country's flag.

Later, in honor of some now-forgotten Soviet holiday, she and her fellow students are told to decorate their classroom. Instead of the expected ornamentation, the students affix garlands of black crepe paper to the ceiling and around windows. Intoxicated by their cleverness and bravado, they laugh while they work, dare each other to take their rebellion further. They place vases of white chrysanthemums on their desks, flowers associated with the dead. The blossoms smell like defiance. On the blackboard, one of the students copies in chalk part of a Latvian poem: "You can bend us, and you can stretch us, but you will never break us." Margrieta takes a moment to read the words, her belief in them a shield.

My mother was in her eighties when she recited that poem fragment to me, her capacity to remember exceptional. It strikes me now that the poet's sentiment applied to much of my mother's life. Throughout our history I often thought of her as broken, and perhaps she was, but some part of her spirit, whatever inspired her to tell these stories, could never be extinguished.

When the school's headmistress discovers what her students have done, she warns them, "Girls, oh girls, please," for she, unlike her charges, understands the danger courted by their disdain. To protect them from the displeasure of visiting Soviet officials, she locks their classroom.

"She was a Communist," my mother said in speaking of the headmistress, "but she was first a Latvian." Her allegiance to the party had grown out of love for her son, a Communist and a Soviet soldier. Later, the German military executed this woman's son and her, for having tried to shield him from being discovered. The outcome was inevitable, my mother said. The German military had warned civilians about the lethal consequences of hiding Soviet soldiers, and yet this woman had no real choice.

I thought my mother's memories of Riga's Central Market—before the war the largest covered market in Europe—exaggerated, a product of nostalgia for Riga before the Soviet takeover. But I confirmed the accuracy of her description of the vast market. It still exists and remains one of the city's major tourist attractions.

Margrieta lived a little over two miles away, so she likely walked there some days, the leather straps of a straw basket in her hand. On the familiar streets, she sometimes lost herself in daydreaming, as you can when you know the way by heart.

I see her wandering the pavilions, where stalls overflow with the bounty of farming, foraging, and fishing. The voices of vendors and shoppers rise and fall, commerce's eager music.

She might stop to sample wild bilberries. Their sweetness bursts in her mouth; the fruit stains her fingers a purplish red. She finds thick honey on the comb, drawn from hives deep in Latvia's dense forests, and mushrooms that smell of dirt and moss. There is pork in all its varieties—from entire pigs to thick slabs of bacon—and fresh and smoked fish. She buys fermented cabbage for sauerkraut, to be savored with apples and brown sugar. Tart cottage cheese and cream so rich it resembles yogurt, the dark, sweet-sour rye bread she likes with butter.

What my mother remembered most about the market wasn't its abundance, but how easily it could be erased. The NKVD pronounced the whole enterprise a hoax designed to showcase a productivity Latvia didn't possess. The Soviets disbanded the market, diverted produce to Russia, and replaced private enterprises with government-controlled stores. "There wasn't any rationing," my mother said, "but you couldn't get food." The only products always available were bread, vodka, hard candy, and Russian wine.

When I was a child in Philadelphia and my mother's father lived with us, he used to take my sister and me on the long walk to the city center and the Eastern European bakery that made a version of the dense Latvian rye bread. And later, my mother sent me to school with a loaf wrapped in a towel and a container of Breakstone's sweet whipped butter, the offering my contribution to a third-grade culinary show-and-tell. I remember thinking bread wasn't special, not like wontons or *gulab jamun*—fried balls of flour and milk soaked in rose-scented syrup, treats a friend's mother made for us. I wished my mother had given me something original or delivered the bread herself, so that she could explain why it mattered.

Margrieta and her parents shared an elegant and spacious apartment within the College of Commerce for which her father served as the director. From its tall windows, she could see the park where she had gone sledding as a little girl. Their home—with its high ceilings and ornamental crown molding, light-filled rooms, parquet floors buffed to a sheen—challenged the NKVD's directives regarding acceptable accommodations for a family of three. Lee had to find a smaller place, one that met the Soviet-imposed limitations of square meters per person, beginning a process of displacement that would become one of the salient characteristics of the war.

When my mother and father bought their first house, the only one they would ever share, I think my mother saw a potential for loveliness that may have reminded her of that Riga apartment. The architectural styles differed, but the house spoke to her. Yet, whatever vision she had for what our family home could become was never realized. That may be why she took such an interest in Tom's and my house in Pittsburgh, at the time the prettiest place I had ever lived.

Among my mother's photographs I found images of our Pittsburgh home, organized in a cardboard folder, "Margaret Tom house" written on the cover. She had retained photos of the backyard in different seasons, the brick walkway curving to the front door, an area we had planted with trees and shrubs to guide visitors to that entrance rather than the door to the laundry room. She had a photo of the enclosed porch I called the sunroom, because of the way sunlight filtered through the branches of surrounding trees to wash the yellow walls in green. The room was not heated, so we used it in spring through autumn. Weekend mornings, Tom and I would read there, our terriers, Gilbert and Annie, snuggled on the sofa between us. Gilbert and Annie lived most of their lives in that sturdy brick Colonial and within the confines of the lush backyard.

Just before Tom and I departed Pittsburgh, I realized that it wasn't the city I would miss, or even our house and garden. I would miss the life we had lived there with our dogs. The house's rooms returned them to me—the family room where Gilbert liked to nap on a corner of the rug warmed by the afternoon sun, his head tucked into his shoulder in a way that always reminded me of a sleeping bird. Descending the stairs to the finished basement, I could see Annie, only four days before she died, running laps around the room, a tiny black-and-white figure moving in her rocking horse way.

In addition to limiting where the family could live and the food available to them, the NKVD's strictures extended to clothing. Margrieta could own two pairs of shoes and a limited number of dresses. All clothing purchases were stamped in her passport: item and date of purchase. "Can you imagine?" my mother asked. "No one owned just two pairs of shoes. We had shoes in different colors."

Winter evenings, after darkness has fallen and she's alone in her cramped bedroom, Margrieta might pull the trunk from under the bed, where she and her mother have hidden their forbidden wardrobe. She holds a soft wool sweater to her cheek, inhales faint traces of perfume, runs her hand over the wide skirt of a silk dress, fingers the strap of a black satin shoe. I doubt she coveted these items as pieces of clothing, fine though they were; she valued them as a promise for the future.

At the gymnasium, Margrieta and her classmates are directed to choose a class president, who will report on students' activities to the NKVD. Most of the students share Margrieta's privileged background, one viewed with hostility by the Soviets, in whose judgment they are plutocrats, affluent members of Latvia's intellectual and cultural elite. The class chooses a girl whose father works in a factory, a background deemed acceptable. *She's our friend*, the students correctly reason, *and she won't spy on us*.

The threat that others, even those once trusted, might betray my mother and her parents never abated. "It became a time when we didn't dare . . . People who had friends on the street crossed the street and pretended they didn't notice them," my mother said.

"The Soviets would tell people—we know about your family, about your activities. We want you to tell us about the activities of your friends," she said. "Many Latvians agreed, thinking they would lie and not tell the Soviets anything. They didn't realize that they had spies behind them too. Spying, spying, spying, spying.

"We believed the NKVD could listen through our phone, even when it wasn't in use," she continued. To protect them from surveillance, Lee put a tea cozy over it, but that would not have conquered their anxiety.

Walking into her apartment building, Margrieta worries the custodian might be an informant. She would be a natural choice for the job—she has access to the entire building and watches who comes and goes. Margrieta learns to mistrust her neighbors, her own judgment. And even more debilitating than the isolation suspicion engenders is the chronic fear, the feeling of dread Stalin inspired. "You were afraid even to dream of him," my mother said. "You hated him, but you feared him like the devil."

The Soviets broke down and frayed social connections. Later, the Germans did the same thing. For both regimes, occupying Latvia required controlling the population through propaganda, coercion, and when deemed more effective, violence. Violence bred cynicism, and that destroyed trust in the goodwill of others.

Margrieta finds comfort in her father's conviction that the Soviet occupation will not last. Paul believes the uneasy alliance between the Soviet Union and Nazi Germany is unsustainable; the two governments have only set aside temporarily their mutual hostility. He predicts Hitler will betray Stalin.

Shortly after the Molotov–Ribbentrop non-aggression pact was signed in the summer of 1939, Germany began repatriating Baltic Germans—evidence, in Paul's opinion, that Hitler planned eventually to attack Russia. "It's only a matter of time," he would say. "When Germany invades Russia, its army will move through Latvia, and we will be liberated."

One late afternoon shortly before German troops occupied Latvia, Paul returned home "absolutely jubilant," my mother said. "The Soviets are leaving," he announced. At Riga's train station he had seen buses, trucks, and freight cars, all empty. Transport, he assumed, for departure.

"That was the real night of horror," my mother said. "The Soviets didn't plan to leave." Soldiers had the names of thousands of Latvians targeted for deportation to distant regions of the Soviet Union—women and children to "administrative settlements" and men to the gulags, the hard labor camps in Siberia.

Over two nights in June 1941, the Soviets exiled some 15,500 Latvians, including 2,400 children younger than ten. They made their arrests at night to disorient the prisoners and avoid alerting others to the threat. A sharp hammering on the targets' door startled the apartment's occupants awake. They were not even given an hour to pack—only what they could carry.

"The soldiers had lists, but if they couldn't meet their quota," my mother said, "they grabbed whomever they found." No one was safe. Soldiers even seized the son of family friends while he was walking home.

"We were not yet caught," she said. "But now we realized that it's only a matter of time." One of Paul's students, a Communist, yet loyal to his beloved teacher, warned Paul that he and his family were now on "the list."

Family friends located a secluded house for rent some fourteen miles from Riga. A vacation home, the house rested on the shores of a lake surrounded by forest. Margrieta and her mother moved there in early summer.

Officially, three women lived at Moon Lake—Margrieta, Lee, and a close family friend, the wife of Riga's chief of police. Unofficially, the police chief and two other male friends also lived there but had to remain hidden. Russian soldiers were searching for Latvian men eligible for military service.

Paul, unlike his friends, believed in his relative safety—he had escaped the first wave of arrests, and the looming German threat made it unlikely the Soviets could manage another. Too old for the Red Army, he didn't fear conscription. He remained in Riga working, unaware his friends had gone into hiding with his family.

Paul learned of their presence the first afternoon he visited but did not have enough time to decide how to deal with the risk.

Some thirty minutes after his arrival, two Russian soldiers knocked on the first of the two sets of doors that served as an entrance to the house. Lee took her time unlocking first the interior and then the exterior door. While she fiddled with the key, she called to the soldiers, urging them to be patient.

Once inside, the soldiers announced that they had received reports of three men hiding within the house, and that they had come to conduct a thorough search. They warned Lee and Paul that if they discovered the men, everyone in the house—the men, now deemed traitors for failure to report for military service, and those who had hidden them—would be shot for treason. To reinforce this threat, machine guns had been set up around the house's perimeter.

Though Paul understood the consequences of discovery and had no idea where the men had hidden themselves, he remained outwardly calm. He smoked his pipe and chatted with the soldiers, telling them he understood their responsibilities and that they should look wherever they felt necessary. Lee pretended to be equally accommodating as she led them on a tour of the house's many rooms, including the attic.

In the meantime, Margrieta feigned sleep in her bedroom. Turned away from the door, she lay on her side, her arms drawn up in front of her chest, her head on the pillow. Waiting. Lee had given her the largest bedroom and decorated it lavishly—Persian rugs on the floor, embroidered pillows on the bed, tapestries on the walls. Behind one of the tapestries stood a door into an antechamber, originally intended as a dressing room or closet. The men huddled silently within.

Lee had reasoned that the soldiers would be reluctant to disturb a young woman sleeping in her bedroom. They would take one look at Margrieta, glance at the room's opulence, and decide the men had to be elsewhere. Her ruse worked, and the soldiers never found the men.

The story of Moon Lake dates from my childhood. Here was a tale of cunning and sangfroid, of daring. The magnitude of the danger only sweetened the thrill of my mother's escape. I identified her as the heroine of this narrative, and the heroine always wins.

Later, upon hearing the anecdote again, I asked my mother if she had feared the soldiers would discover their friends. "The men were hidden. That was that," she said. She went on to tell me that throughout the war she'd believed she would evade all the threats she encountered. Her survival, at least in a psychological sense, depended on constructing a narrative that offered hope.

I tried to learn more about Moon Lake, the cherished setting for my mother's summer between one armed occupation and the next, but when I searched online for lakes near Riga, I could not find it. A Cloud Lake exists, so perhaps my mother's memory was confused, though she remembered identifying details of other locales. I look for some deeper meaning in her mistake. Is Moon Lake a metaphor of desire for some imaginary place, something dreamed of but impossible to reach? It may be, but perhaps not for my mother. That metaphor has more relevance for me. I am the one who longs for intimacy with her, even now after her death.

As my grandfather had predicted, Nazi Germany attacked the Soviet Union in June 1941. By July 10, German armed forces occupied all of Latvia's territory.

Margrieta and Lee could have returned to Riga, but they decided to stay at Moon Lake through summer; the place was so inviting it seemed a shame to give it up before autumn.

One night, a loud knocking awakens Margrieta. Her mother and the others have gone to Riga to assess circumstances there, so she is alone in the house. By then, the invading German forces have driven the Red Army from the area. More curious than frightened, she goes downstairs to investigate. She opens the door to a German officer and three corporals.

The officer bows slightly and asks Margrieta to pardon the intrusion. He merely needs directions and then will disturb her no further. She notices his elegant posture, the warmth in his eyes. *He's handsome*, she thinks, *and not so much older than me*. The night air smells of pine and wet leaves. The light from the full moon paints the surrounding forest silver.

"And there I was, a pretty young girl with war-grimed soldiers. I invited them in and offered them drinks. They were perfect gentlemen, absolutely perfect gentlemen," my mother said.

I asked if she'd been afraid to be alone with the soldiers.

"No, I wasn't afraid at all. Maybe I was very naive, but I assumed they'd be fine. They were our friends. They'd liberated us." My mother believed the German Army had saved her parents and her from exile and probable death. Having rid the country of the Soviets, they had also ignited hope that Latvia might regain its independence.

"And I must say this for the German Army," she continued, "because in the Second World War, I saw them all. I saw Americans, Canadians, Russians, British . . . The best-behaved army, the most gentlemanly army for civilians, is the German Army."

I cannot think of the German Army without thinking of the Holocaust, and in this, my mother and I differed. When I pressed her about the Wehrmacht's complicity, even if passive, in what became known as crimes against humanity, she insisted, "They did not kill Jews. They did not approve of it. They abhorred it. You could blame them for not turning against the SS, but not for other things."

She made a distinction between the Wehrmacht, the combined armed forces responsible for combat operations, and the SS. The latter was charged with maintaining Germany's internal security and promoting racial purity within a Greater Germany. The SS reported, via Himmler, directly to Hitler, and considered itself superior to Germany's other forces. My mother reminded me that Wehrmacht officers did not associate with the SS. "There were restaurants in Riga," she said, "where only the SS could go. A German general would not be admitted."

Her personal experience with German officers informed her impressions of the army, starting with the young officer who knocked on the door of the house that night.

My mother characterized her monthlong romance with Eric, which ended when he was transferred to the Russian front, as "a rather juvenile love affair . . . very idealistic." But how could it have been otherwise? Meeting Eric after the Soviet occupation—a time Latvians would call "the year of horror"—must have felt like emerging from a dark, frigid room into sunlight.

I never lived under the weight of Soviet oppression, never had my freedom curtailed in the ways my mother experienced, nor faced the threats the Soviet regime imposed on those deemed enemies of the people. But I remember myself at eighteen. I embarked on a love affair I might now describe as immature and unrealistic, but no less intense for those limitations. In fact, the obstacles to our romance—his Jewish faith that precluded a long-term relationship with me, and our shared youth and inexperience—increased our fascination with each other. And like my mother, I'd not had any serious boyfriends while in high school, so the newness of it all contributed to our ardor.

I imagine Margrieta giddy with the excitement of first love. Her world grown larger and brighter in Eric's company. They enjoyed evenings of dinners and concerts, long walks in the twilight under spreading trees. Eric told her about his native Düsseldorf, promised her he would show her his city. And she daydreamed about going there with him. Both forgetting about the war for a time, believing themselves immune from its brutality.

When I asked my mother about the greatest changes under the German occupation, she said, "Freedom and loss of anguish, no fear anymore."

The Nazis sought to sustain the perception that they had liberated Latvia and that cooperation with the occupying forces would result in the restoration of Latvia's sovereignty. In fact, the Third Reich intended to subsume Latvia within a Greater Germany in service of *lebensraum*, living space for the growing German race. Paul recognized this, but he still preferred German to Soviet occupation because the former gave Latvia more time. "Latvia will perish as a nation in one year under Stalin, and in seven years under Hitler," he said. My grandfather did not view the German occupation favorably. It represented the lesser evil.

In autumn Margrieta and Lee departed Moon Lake to return to Riga, where living conditions had improved. Though the Germans imposed a rationing system, far more food was available. A black market emerged, within which the Germans tolerated modest violations. Because they had friends in the countryside, Margrieta and her parents could get bacon and smoked pork. When she wanted cream, a product reserved for the military, she got one of her professors to give her a prescription claiming she had tuberculosis and needed to enrich her diet.

Thanks to Lee's friendship with an Austrian officer, Margrieta and her parents eventually moved to a new apartment. Rudi had been assigned spacious quarters in the same building, just across a common courtyard. When he saw their spartan accommodations—the place they had been forced to take during the Soviet occupation—he offered to switch apartments.

Tony Judt, in his *Postwar: A History of Europe Since 1945*, notes that living normally in occupied Europe required breaking the law—first the laws of the occupiers but also conventional laws and norms. My mother and her parents manipulated the constraints of the occupation and benefited from the generosity of one Austrian officer. That did not make them supporters of the Nazi regime and its murderous agenda. It made them ordinary people living as best they could under an army of occupation. I do not judge their behavior. I recognize its pragmatism.

After the war, my mother learned that her Latvian boyfriend from that time, an artist, was half Jewish. Eventually conscripted into the German Army, he hid his identity to fight for the Third Reich. I cannot know the calculus he made, and some would argue that he betrayed his faith and ethnicity, but he likely had no choice if he wanted to live.

The Third Reich guarded as secret its plans to annihilate Jews and others deemed subhuman, so the degree to which most Latvians recognized the extent of Nazi viciousness remains unclear, and the boundaries between guilt, non-involvement, and resistance cloudy. Nevertheless, I struggled to understand how my mother had failed to recognize the genocide underway in her native Riga.

"At the beginning of the German occupation," my mother said, "it seemed like everything was quiet and nothing particular happened. Then they started to line up Communists. They sent them fourteen miles out of Riga to a concentration camp. The people were just concentrated there, held in detention. That was the general information." Among those confined were many Jews, but she believed they had been detained because of politics, not ethnicity. *Oh, they are Communists*, she thought at the time. *Serves them right.*

I remind myself that my mother was eighteen at the beginning of the German occupation. Engaged in a rigorous academic program in medicine and romantically involved with her Latvian artist, she didn't look beyond those concerns. She remembered life under the Soviets as a time of grinding fear. To the extent that my mother evaluated the German occupation, she did so in comparison with what had preceded it.

My grandmother also focused on the personal, preoccupied with concerns that touched that circumscribed world. Only my grandfather, a student of history and an astute observer of political life, felt compelled to look at the larger forces shaping his country. But even for him, access to information was neither timely nor facile.

Paul started to suspect that the Nazis were targeting Jews when a colleague shared his worry about his daughter, who was married to a Jewish man. He had advised her to divorce her husband. "He had information," my mother said, "that Jews will be lined up and sent to the concentration camp, and if she is not divorced, she will be sent with him." The daughter refused and her future unfolded as her father had feared.

Another incident reinforced Paul's suspicions. A Jewish professor and his wife lived in the same apartment building as Paul and Lee. The professor's wife invited Lee and Margrieta for a visit, during which she asked Lee to take her family silver and other valuables for safekeeping. She expected to be sent with her husband to Riga's concentration camp, where, she assumed, they would await deportation to their native Poland. Even this woman, though persecuted, failed to perceive the magnitude of the threat.

Lee considered obliging her, but Paul "absolutely forbade it," my mother said. When I asked why, she told me that he didn't accept their neighbor's hypothesis. It made no sense for the Germans to return anyone to Poland; people were fleeing Poland. "Once she is gone, she will be gone," Paul said, "and I am not going to become enriched by someone else's loss."

Within six months of the Nazi occupation, the majority of Latvia's Jews had been killed. The largest single massacre—occurring between the Babi Yar killings in Ukraine and the establishment of Nazi extermination camps—took place over two days in late November and early December 1941 in the Rumbula forest, about nine miles south of Riga. Approximately twenty-five thousand Jews were murdered.

Later, as the war started to turn against Germany and the Red Army advanced toward the Latvian border, the Germans forced prisoners to reopen the mass graves and burn the corpses to destroy evidence of their crimes.

"And the smoke on the horizon was something horrible. It was so horrible. My father locked himself in his room and was in an absolute black, black mood," my mother said. "But I didn't accept it at all. I had a fine time being entertained by German officers."

I heard the regret in my mother's voice when she recalled that time. I wonder if at her age—she was twenty-one in 1944—I would have behaved in a similar way, difficult as it is for me to conjure the world in which she lived. I suspect that like my mother, I would have pursued pleasure where I found it. The violence and cruelty infecting her country did not affect her or anyone she knew personally, and without that association, it was easier to remain ignorant.

"I separated myself totally from what was happening in Riga," my mother explained. Her feelings of guilt emerged later when she remembered her father's struggle. "He suffered while all of this was happening." Paul couldn't distance himself, even if the terror did not engulf him personally. "Why here?" he'd groan. "Why does such a thing have to happen in Latvia?" I believe I understand what he meant, but I have a question, one that I recognize as unfair even as I raise it. It reveals more about me and my ambivalent feelings toward my grandfather than it does about him. I want to ask him what bothered him more—*what* happened or *where* it happened?

My mother, speaking of her own reaction, said, "The thing is, my own attitude . . . it's hard to explain. You know when the Holocaust happened and all the pictures were shown later on television, about the corpses in the concentration camps. I didn't doubt that they were genuine. But somehow it was surreal. It was too horrible to grasp, really." It was as if it happened on "another planet," she said. And how could it be otherwise? The scale of the Holocaust still remains unimaginable to me. Only when I find a personal connection to it does it become something tangible.

Though there had been a significant Jewish minority living in Riga, a community that prospered before the war started, my mother did not have any Jewish friends. The Jewish community, at least the observant Jews within it, did not mingle with Christians. At the same time, my mother assured me, there wasn't any prejudice toward them. After the Nuremberg Laws of 1935 denied German Jews citizenship, Latvia welcomed those who wished to immigrate. "They thought they'd be safe here," my mother said.

My mother's perspective changed after she had been living in the United States for a time. We had Jewish friends, for whom the Holocaust held personal meaning, and by a kind of social osmosis, some of that understanding passed to my mother and me. Yet, when it came to talking about her heightened awareness of the war's atrocities, she credited a television miniseries and a novel.

Holocaust, broadcast in 1978, follows members of a prominent Jewish family as each falls victim to Hitler's Germany. The film portrays people with whom my mother identified. "That was the first time when I really grasped the whole horror."

Frederick Forsyth's 1972 novel *The Odessa File* draws from historical fact concerning the mass murders engineered by SS Captain Eduard Roschmann, administrator of the Riga Ghetto, and later known as "The Butcher of Riga." My mother recognized street names and other details about her birthplace, descriptions that placed her back in time. And the novel made her remember something else: "I had been together socially with one of the supervisors of the concentration camp in Riga without knowing who he was," she said.

My mother encountered him at a party given by Riga's chief of police, one of the men the family had sheltered at Moon Lake. The police chief, like other civil servants, was responsible for billeting and entertaining German officers, including this SS captain. My young mother wouldn't have questioned his presence at the party nor sought to understand his responsibilities. He impressed her then as charming and cultured. And though I resist acknowledging this, I'm sure he was appealing in that setting. I picture him self-assured and at ease in the living room of the police chief's home, a glass of champagne in his hand, an attentive expression on his face, as he chats with the other guests.

Only years later did my mother recognize that the courteous officer whose company she had enjoyed was a mass murderer. I heard her disbelief but didn't ask her what she struggled to accept. That she had brushed up against evil without recognizing it and perhaps not for the first time? Or that her favorable response to this man made her somehow complicit?

When I was growing up, my mother rarely mentioned Latvia or introduced me to Baltic culture. I associated amber, woodlands of white birch trees, smoked fish, rye bread, and not much more with her birthplace. Instead of saying she was Latvian, she would more often say, "I am European," claiming Europe as the region and culture to which she belonged. I see in her assertion a subtle denial of her native land. And also, it seems to me now, shame.

Tony Judt wrote that for most Europeans, the Second World War was experienced not as a war of movement and battle but as a daily degradation, in which everyone lost something and many lost everything.

My mother lost her country. Twice. First to the Soviet Union, as that regime sought to erase Latvia—the country's people and history, even its language. And second, in a more complicated way, and as a result of the war's legacy, to memory.

Latvia finally regained its independence from the Soviet Union on August 21, 1991, fifty-two years after the execution of the Molotov–Ribbentrop Pact. My mother never expressed any desire to visit, though she was pleased that her country had finally exorcised the Soviets, or at least created the possibility of such an exorcism.

Until recently, I did not have much interest in seeing Latvia, but now I want to travel there. I would like to recover something I have only now learned to miss.

A Terrible Peace

I see Margrieta on the train bound for Vienna in the early summer of 1944, shortly before the Russian Army's reoccupation of Latvia. This is the second time she is leaving Riga to escape the Soviets, but unlike that summer at Moon Lake, perhaps she knows she will not return.

Rudi, the Austrian officer who exchanged apartments with Lee and is now her lover, has arranged their transport and provided documents claiming Margrieta and Lee are ethnic Germans seeking repatriation. Vienna isn't open to refugees, so that distinction—that small lie in their identification papers—makes the difference.

When Margrieta and Lee departed Riga, Paul remained behind. He finally fled on one of the last ships to leave Latvia before the Soviet reoccupation. He spent the rest of the war in a refugee camp in Germany.

Sunlight from Hotel Bristol's arched windows washes over the marble floors. The room smells of coffee and cigarettes. Margrieta fingers the delicate handle of her coffee cup, brushes breadcrumbs from the crisp white tablecloth. She only half listens to her mother's conversation. They have encountered Latvian friends from Riga, and everyone is eager to prolong the illusion of being in Vienna on holiday. The city itself contributes to the fantasy. Early German victories and Vienna's geographic placement beyond the range of Allied bombers have thus far spared the Viennese the full realization of the war.

Lee chatters away, a brightness in her voice that sounds like happiness. Rudi has divorced his Austrian wife and wants to marry her. Margrieta does not choose sides between her parents—she never did, not even as a small child. She is relieved her mother has found Rudi. Perhaps their love affair will calm Lee's volatile temper, for which she has so often been the target.

Margrieta and her mother decide to enjoy this bubble of luxury. The Germans are losing the war and their money will soon be worthless, so why not spend it? They book a suite for two weeks.

Vienna, a city so much larger and more cosmopolitan than Riga, enchants Margrieta. She strolls the Ringstrasse, the ring road that girdles Vienna's historic center. She might pause to admire the Vienna Opera, its ornate grandeur best appreciated from a distance. The building's high dome gleams in the morning sunshine.

She says, years later, that she had always believed she belonged somewhere other than Latvia, finding that world too provincial for her aspirations. For the rest of her life, she will speak of Vienna and the Viennese with love.

The war has not extinguished Margrieta's hopes of becoming a doctor. Before fleeing Riga, she completed six terms at the University of Latvia, Medical Faculty, Department of Dentistry.

The director of admissions had promised she could transfer from dentistry to medicine after the first year, if her grades were good. She achieved excellent grades, but the director didn't honor his commitment, most likely because of a grudge he held against her father. Because prospective dentists and doctors pursued the same course of study for the first two years, Margrieta's training positions her to work at a Vienna hospital specializing in reconstructive maxillofacial surgery.

One night, traveling home to the apartment she shares with her mother in the suburbs, she falls asleep on the train. Grateful to sit down, after having stood for hours assisting in surgeries, she doesn't intend to sleep, only to close her eyes for a few minutes. The train's rocking soothes her as it trundles down the track toward the countryside. The dark cold outside makes the car's interior feel warmer, and she sleeps heavily. She misses her stop and does not awaken until the conductor shakes her shoulder. There isn't any negotiating with him; she must leave the train. She stumbles outside into frigid blackness and begins walking, her breath forming clouds before it freezes on her face. The wind and the ice crunching beneath her boots, the only sounds she hears. She fears she will freeze to death if she doesn't find shelter. She knows what that would be like: pain at first—in her fingers and toes, the tip of her nose—before a loss of feeling, the absence of pain a signal that parts of her body are beginning to die. Finally, an overwhelming drowsiness, tempting her to lie down in the snow. She would tell herself it was only to gain some strength, and that would be the last thing she remembered.

In the darkness, she sees the light of the train warden's hut and trudges toward it. She bangs on the door and a man opens it to her. He looks to be in his late fifties, his face lined, cheeks unshaven, watery blue eyes. He doesn't smile, confused and irritated at being disturbed. He doesn't invite her in, but she steps around him into the small room while she explains that she has missed her stop. There will not be another train until morning and his is the only dwelling around. He insists she leave because an inspector will check to confirm he is alone. He has only this one room and the alcove behind the curtain, where his bed sits. She begs him to let her stay, telling him she cannot survive the cold outside. His silence gives way to acceptance. He directs her to hide in the alcove until the inspector has come and gone.

She lies down on the small metal bed, hears the inspector confirm that the train yard is secure. After he departs, the warden tells her she can go to sleep. He'll spend the night in his chair. She tries to rest, but she feels guilty about the warden, who's also tired, sitting up all night. She offers to share his bed; after all, she's wearing a coat and hat, gloves. She moves close to the wall to give him room. He settles himself on the straw-filled mattress, pulls the wool blanket over them both. She is still so tired and only wants to rest.

In the middle of the night, she feels his hand on her breast. He's lying on his side and nuzzling her neck, his unshaven cheek scraping her skin. Fully awake now, she starts to cry. He doesn't expect her tears. He apologizes and explains he didn't want to frighten her. They spend the remainder of the night peacefully.

When my mother described this incident, she emphasized the risk of freezing to death and remembered the train warden as the person who had given her shelter. She did not interpret his offensive behavior as sexual assault. Not long afterward he sent her a letter, so she must have told him where he could find her. He called her a "Madonna, a saint," a woman of such purity that he remained in awe of her. She found it amusing.

My mother set a low bar for male behavior when it came to unwanted sexual advances. She viewed such behavior as a burden to be managed if she wanted to navigate a world dominated by men.

In one of our later conversations, I talked to my mother about her work as a doctor. When she first arrived in the United

States, she managed to secure an internship at Methodist Episcopal Hospital in South Philadelphia. Her supervisor, a more senior physician, grabbed her breasts during a physical exam. Thereafter, whenever he found her alone, he persisted in his predatory behavior. She successfully resisted his advances, and she didn't report the assault, not initially. When she eventually spoke to the department chair, she only did so because she had learned that her supervisor, in what I assume was retaliation for refusing him, was trying to get her fired. The department chair dealt with him, warning him that he would be dismissed if there were any additional complaints.

My mother revealed the assault and harassment because her job, rather than her person, had been threatened. When I asked her what she would advise me to do in the event of sexual aggression in the workplace, her immediate response was, "It depends." I would have to weigh the costs of confronting power. That calculus, sadly, is still being made by women.

Margrieta is working in the operating room when she hears the siren's wail. She feels the familiar dread and must suppress the urge to add her voice to the horn's screams. She fears that if she starts, she won't be able to stop. A cuckoo's two-note call follows, warning her that this air raid will last longer and be more extensive. Allied bombing raids are possible now in this last year of war, as the Allied invasion of Italy has placed American long-range bombers within striking distance of Vienna. The hospital lies near an industrial area, targeted for attack.

She focuses on the surgeon's instructions; they calm her. *We can't leave the patient*, she tells herself. *We must take courage from each other.*

In the end, my mother's adopted city did not escape the war's destruction. Bombs gutted Vienna—killing civilians, destroying homes, damaging electric lines, as well as sewer, gas, and water pipes. I never asked my mother about these conditions and the hardship they created, though now I wish I had. Without her descriptions, I am left to conjure her environment.

She walks Vienna's streets, careful to avoid bomb craters and bodies, some of which are still recognizable as human. She ties a scarf around her face, but the stench of corruption still threatens to overwhelm her. *Keep walking*, she tells herself. *There's nothing you can do. Be grateful you're still alive.*

During those final months of the war in Europe, Margrieta and Lee lived in Vienna's historic center, house-sitting for Dr. Walters, an oral surgeon and Margrieta's supervisor. He'd been recalled to military service. His apartment stood on a street perpendicular to the Ringstrasse. From its tall windows, Margrieta watched the Vienna Opera burn, set ablaze by bombs that had landed nearby. Flames destroyed the auditorium and the stage—she could feel the fire's heat in the rippling air. To prevent smoldering debris from igniting the apartment, she put pans of water on the windowsills. The Opera, a place akin to Vienna's heart, burned for twenty hours.

I have a photograph of Dr. Walters, on the back of which my mother wrote, "I almost married the guy." A widower in his early forties, he was some twenty years older. I can guess at my mother's effect on him—a man who had seen the carnage of war and tried to mitigate the suffering it had caused. Here before him, Margrieta, with her golden hair and clear green eyes, a color reminiscent of seawater.

In the photograph, Josef wears a suit that looks expensive, given how it hugs his shoulders. Under the suit jacket an immaculate shirt with French cuffs, a folded handkerchief in his breast pocket. He reminds me of Errol Flynn, the same thick dark hair and eyes, even a carefully groomed mustache.

His arms are folded in front of him; his manicured nails have been buffed recently. Everything about him suggests meticulous grooming. And wealth.

Josef smiles at the camera, but his eyes remain somber. His wife, Maria, an accomplished fashion designer, is dead. Perhaps he is thinking of her.

Slipping into the role of wife to this cultured and successful Austrian tempts Margrieta. Maria's clothes, still hanging in the apartment's closets, fit her. Perhaps the life would as well. Wherever she wanders in Josef's home, she finds evidence of his privilege—in the fine furnishings, bookcases lined with leather-bound volumes, the feel of soft linens. While others struggle to survive with ration cards, she has enough to eat—the benefits of a still-sufficient larder.

Josef offers Margrieta security at a time when the cumulative effects of the war's deprivations and destruction are starting to gnaw away at her confidence in the future. In Vienna's streets, she tries not to see the women sifting through rubble in search of something of value, or the older men who walk miles, scouring forests for firewood. She averts her gaze from these desperate people, afraid she will recognize their hopelessness.

My mother might have settled for what would have likely been a comfortable, stable, and affectionate marriage. I'm glad she didn't, because had she married Josef, she would not have become my mother. But it's more than that. I understand how easily she could have embraced the life he offered. I wonder what I would have chosen if faced with the same stark choice between a future that seemed knowable and safe, and one increasingly uncertain. I like to think I would have placed my hopes in the latter, as my mother ultimately did.

Other aspects of Josef's appeal resonate with me, because he fit the profile I once devised for a future husband: older and more mature; professionally accomplished; cultured; and, also, European. In my case, however, my ideal husband came from fiction.

When I was thirteen or so, my mother introduced me to *Came a Cavalier*, a 1947 novel by Frances Parkinson Keyes. Keyes's protagonist, Constance Galt, is an American working for the Red Cross in France during the final months of the First World War. She meets, falls in love with, and agrees to marry a French nobleman and cavalry officer. From the moment Tristan de Fremont is introduced on the page, he is irresistible. Tall, dark, and handsome—of course—but also erudite and in possession of impeccable manners. He pursues Constance with sensitivity and impressive persistence. She finally succumbs, as the reader knows she will. Together, they build a radiant life in Normandy of sufficient depth and resiliency to carry them through the inevitable separations and sorrows of the Second World War.

Consider my surprise when I fell in love with a blond, blue-eyed, younger American, and without any of the trappings of sophistication I believed were essential. Truth be told, I wasn't the shrewd judge of such things I pretended to be. Still, I fancied myself more worldly than Tom in virtually every way. Given this bias, for the first few months after our initial meeting, I persisted in viewing Tom as no more than a friend and continued to interpret his gestures through that lens.

Early in our first semester at Wharton, Tom arranged a birthday dinner for me with friends at an Italian restaurant in South Philadelphia. He had gone so far as to get me a gift and bake a birthday cake. I remember the lovely Irish wool sweater in pink with contrasting shades of deeper rose and lavender at the neckline. I didn't think of it at the time, but giving me that present likely meant Tom did without something else, as his finances were stretched thin by Wharton's hefty tuition bill. When I showed the sweater to my sister, she commented that it didn't look like a gift from a friend.

There was a German wartime joke, one my mother repeated to me: "Better enjoy the war—the peace will be terrible."

The Red Army was the first to enter Vienna in April 1945, and they controlled the city until the other Allies arrived. According to medical reports cited by Tony Judt in *Postwar*, some eighty-seven thousand women in Vienna were raped by Soviet soldiers in the first three weeks of the Red Army's occupation. My mother was among them, based on stories she told others, though she never revealed the attack to me. I know only of a narrow escape.

Margrieta takes a wool jacket from the closet, holds it against her body, confident it will fit, as the dresses have, now piled on the bed like so many women sleeping. She strokes the cashmere fabric, runs her fingers lightly over the brass buttons. So finely crafted—this jacket Maria once wore, sewn according to her own design—one of the many garments Josef has given her.

She lays the jacket on the bed, pauses for a moment, and looks toward the windows that face the Ringstrasse. The afternoon light on the wooden floors reveals cracks in some places, and she wonders why she hadn't noticed them during the weeks she has been living here. She thinks of Josef, still away tending to wounded German soldiers, who are now prisoners of war.

Maybe it's that thought—of damaged men, men who will never recover who they'd once been—that makes her sad. Or maybe it's having to leave the apartment, displaced once more, because Josef's sister-in-law resents her presence there. She inhales the musty odor of silk curtains, the silence. Her hands feel cold. She wants to finish packing, so she can leave. But where is her mother? She should have returned by now.

Her back to the bedroom's threshold, she doesn't hear the Russian soldier enter the apartment. When she turns, he's there. She gasps and clenches her hands, her only weapon. The soldier stands silent, on his face a look of wonder.

Margrieta sees herself gliding past him and out the door. If she behaves with enough authority, he might let her go. But the moment passes. He wants to know what she is doing. "Packing my clothes," she tells him. "I'll be finished soon and then I won't bother you anymore." A hot wire of resentment pulses in her chest. She has more right to be here than he, but she can't let him see her anger, because he will respond in kind. He takes a few steps forward, scanning the room, before his eyes return to her. Margrieta considers running, but he'd stop her. She's sure of that now. And then he'd have his hands on her.

He points to the bed and laughs as if they are sharing a joke. She knows what he wants, but he isn't threatening her, not yet. *I need to stall for time, time enough for my mother to get back*, she thinks. She makes herself smile at this Russian and tells him that such a handsome man has no reason to force himself on her. There will be many women who will want him if he can only be patient. She feels the tremor in her voice and hopes he doesn't hear her fear. That would make this worse somehow. *What can I say to persuade him to let me go?* He steps closer and the spacious room suddenly feels like a cell.

Russian voices reverberate in the hallway. Margrieta feels her heart hammering, as if to escape her chest. Her palms sweat and she wipes them on her skirt. She looks to the door again, willing her mother to walk in, but the entrance is now blocked by olive green and flashes of red. She can't see beyond the soldiers. *How many of them are there?*

A voice calls out, "Anton," but the man standing in front of her only grunts a reply. He doesn't take his eyes from her. She sees something change in his expression, a hardening. "Please," she says, but Anton is now part of a pack. She thinks of wolves.

There is no point in fighting. I don't have the strength and there are too many. As he moves toward her, she hears her mother's voice. Lee is screaming at the soldiers, trying to force her way into the room. The Russians laugh and push her back into the hallway. They keep their focus on Margrieta.

Desperate to gain a little more time, Margrieta calls the Russian by his name, hoping to make him return to himself. She tells him she will give him what he wants, but only him. She wants him to make the others leave so that they can be alone. "We don't have to hurry," she says. "Let me take these things from the bed." He watches her as she starts moving the dresses to the floor.

My mother told me that Lee, frantic to save her, ran out into the street crowded with Soviet soldiers. She stood in front of a Soviet tank until she got an officer's attention. Perhaps because she spoke Russian, he listened to her. Perhaps when she begged him to help, he thought of his own child and softened. In any case, he followed her to the apartment, ordered the soldiers to disperse, and escorted Lee and my mother from the building.

Or maybe that's not what happened. In another version of this story, one my mother told others, four Russian soldiers raped her. Her mother tried to save her, clawing at the men like a wild animal, but they only laughed and pushed her away. Lee risked being raped herself, but perhaps her fury dissuaded them. Or maybe my grandmother's rape is a story I never heard.

My mother dismissed the attack as part of the war's reality. "What do you expect?" she'd say. "It was wartime and these men wanted a woman." Afterward, they offered her gifts—cigarettes and chocolate. I understand my mother's reaction, because, in reality, what recourse did she have to hold these men to account? She would not have seen any value in dwelling on what could not be changed. She had survived.

When I spoke to my mother about what happened in that Vienna apartment, I feared she would tell me she had been raped. But she didn't. And I did not ask the explicit question then that I might ask now: Were you *ever* raped in

Vienna? If I had, she would have told me the truth. I avoided the question because I didn't want to revive old wounds; she'd already revealed so much. But perhaps I also wanted to safeguard the narrative I preferred, the one in which my grandmother saves my mother.

Once the Americans arrived in Vienna, some threats Margrieta faced diminished, while others intensified. The Allies divided Austria into four zones of occupation, three of which were assigned to the major Allied powers—the United States, the Soviet Union, and the United Kingdom—and the fourth, a smaller area, to France. The Soviet Union occupied the eastern part of Austria, except for Vienna, which was also divided into four zones. The Allies declared the central historical district, where Margrieta lived, an international zone, for which the occupation forces changed on a monthly basis.

To avoid repatriation to the Soviet Union, Margrieta needed false identity papers, claiming she had been born in Austria and was an Austrian citizen. The stories around those papers remain unclear to me, except one point. My mother told me that the person who provided the documents never asked for anything in return. Her enduring affection for the Viennese may have originated there. She had faith in a fundamental kindness she found among these Austrians. She reminded me that there were many times when Austrian acquaintances could have denounced her as a Soviet citizen, but they never did.

Margrieta's papers reported her birthplace as Graz, Austria, a town she didn't know. If questioned about her background, she wouldn't have been convincing in her lies. She had to avoid interrogation. When she traveled through the Soviet zone by train, before boarding she would drink enough wine to be convincingly, if not actually, drunk. After pinning her documents to her coat, she would pretend to sleep, hoping that the Soviet inspectors would glance at the papers and not bother to rouse her from an alcohol-induced slumber.

Survival in Vienna depended on access to the black market, despite the scarcity of food available there; participating in it, however, was illegal. The Soviets used investigations into violations as a pretext to locate former citizens. During the month when the Russians controlled the historical district, they searched wherever they wanted, including Margrieta's apartment building, supposedly looking for contraband. Like most people, she had things acquired on the black market, cigarettes or whatever. If the NKVD discovered the illegal items, they'd haul her back to the *Kommandatura*, Soviet military headquarters, where they could scrutinize her papers and interrogate her.

A neighbor knocks on the apartment door and warns her that she saw the NKVD enter the building. Margrieta hurries from the apartment and makes her way to the basement—a room of stone walls with an earthen floor, the place damp and smelling of mold. She has hidden in other basements, even the catacombs of St. Stephen's Cathedral during Allied bombing raids. Most terrifying were the bombs that fell near the building—the surrounding pressure made her fear the walls would buckle inward, burying her alive. She is afraid now too, also of being buried alive, because if the Soviets find her and she cannot somehow negotiate her freedom, she understands that her life will become a kind of living death.

She sits on the floor, her back against the wall, hugging herself against the chill, focusing on believing she is safe, because she cannot succumb to fear. Her fear would give her away, if not this time, then the next.

I have a copy of an article about my mother published in Pennsylvania's *Chester Times* in 1951, two years after her arrival in the United States. The Cold War, already underway, created interest in accounts of life in the Soviet Union, and my mother agreed to an interview. The article's title, "Yule Cards Bring Horror Not Joy Behind Iron Curtain," foregrounds my mother's description of the NKVD's threatening response to a Christmas card her father received from a friend in the West during the first Soviet occupation of Latvia. Having contacts in the West made my grandfather the target of an intense investigation and put his life in danger. She went on to talk about the Soviets' abuse of those they deemed threats—confining prisoners in rooms covered in mirrors or infuriating color combinations, cubicles so cramped the person had to remain in a crouched position. She spoke about children being taken from their homes for questioning. When returned to their parents, they appeared terrified and refused to speak about what had happened.

My mother knew what awaited her should the Soviets find her in Vienna. The Russians promised revenge against all who had escaped their rule. They would find those who had fled, even if it took fifty years.

Fear of the Soviets colored my mother's years in Vienna, but not always as the dominant hue. The character of that time was also defined by her passionate engagement with her own life, an intense vitality I never saw.

My mother arrived in Austria when she was twenty-one, naive and in most ways still a girl. She departed at age twenty-seven, a young woman intent on her future in the United States. Those six years matured her, sometimes in painful ways. But as my mother used to say, usually in response to some unwanted but necessary life lesson, "School costs money."

When I consider a similar time period in my own life, I do not find anything as dramatic as my mother's experience. At twenty-two, I lived in the United States during a time of peace. I had recently graduated from the University of Pennsylvania and was working full-time, but not in a job I wanted to keep. I did not have the resources to move out of my parents' home. I had been infatuated with a few young men, but never in love. I was searching—personally, professionally, and in other ways I could not have named.

By my twenty-seventh birthday, my father had been dead for more than two years, a sudden loss that accelerated change within my family and pushed me toward making my own decisions about the future. I was in my third semester of business school, a choice more practical than inspired, but, nevertheless, sound. Tom and I had been together for a year and were headed toward marriage. If you had asked me about the future, I would have told you I had a clear plan and that I did not doubt its achievement. Though my twenty-seven-year-old mother and I differed in many ways, we shared one characteristic: our certainty.

In November of 1945, after the universities reopened, Margrieta talked her way into medical school, achieving in Vienna what had not been possible in Riga. The University of Vienna initially refused to consider her application, claiming that as a stateless person, she couldn't find a home in medicine. She persisted in pleading her case until the director of admissions relented.

Her academic records from the University of Latvia confirmed that she had completed six terms as a student in the Medical Faculty, Department of Dentistry. She had to translate these documents into German and did so word for word with one exception: She omitted the reference to the Department of Dentistry.

Years later, remembering the gamble she had taken, my mother said, "I gave the University of Vienna my original records, along with my translation. They could have seen the change I'd made." Apparently, they didn't, and she was admitted as a second-year student in a five-year program, though the University of Vienna allowed students to take much longer to complete their studies if they wanted. "You could finish medical school in five or twenty years," she said. That flexibility ultimately created problems for her when she sought to have her Austrian credentials recognized in the United States.

When I first heard this story of my mother's maneuver, I couldn't decide whether I found it deceptive or resourceful. I think now that it was both. My mother relied on subterfuge to survive during the war—pretending to be Austrian rather than Latvian—but later, too, in more subtle ways, when she revised aspects of her history to make it bearable.

My mother and Lee lived apart in Austria, for the first time in my mother's life, and that separation must have felt like freedom. She no longer had to navigate Lee's moods to avoid being submerged by them. She told me that as a child she never invited any friends home, because she never knew which version of her mother she might find.

A significant friendship developed for my mother in Vienna, a relationship made possible because she was not living with Lee. My mother met Marga, another Latvian displaced by the war, on a Vienna street one hot summer day. She first noticed Marga's attire—a blue dirndl dress, much too short for her, and ski boots. In my imagination, Marga also drags with her a large suitcase, her worldly possessions. "She looked ridiculous," my mother told me.

Marga needed a place to live, so my mother invited her to share her apartment. I have the sense that Marga looked after my mother. She worked in administration for the American hotel and club section and introduced my mother to Americans, expanding her social life. She also protected my mother from encounters with Russian soldiers. If my mother was out late, Marga would send an American soldier with a jeep to drive her home.

After Marga and my mother both immigrated to the United States—Marga to California and my mother to Pennsylvania—they didn't have much contact, though Marga did visit once. I found a photograph of the two of them taken during the afternoon they spent together. In the photo, Marga is still the "big girl" my mother remembered from Vienna: "hefty, but not fat." She has an open face, not pretty in a conventional way, yet friendly. She looks like someone I'd like to know. My mother and her friend smile toward the camera and seem to be having a good time.

In parting, Marga told me that I needed to help my mother. I understood she didn't mean with the housework, but something more complicated. At the same time, I remember thinking, *I'm only twelve years old. Shouldn't my mother be helping me, rather than the other way around?* I realize now that Marga had seen something worrisome in my mother's demeanor. A deepening sadness or some new fragility.

From my mother's years in Vienna, I find another loose photograph, an image of Dr. Boch, a professor of literature at the University of Vienna. He acted as guardian for Tamara Petersen, one of my mother's friends from Riga, so she must have met him through Tamara. His cultured and hospitable home offered my mother a refuge. Not in a physical sense, but as a reminder that the world still held the possibility of grace.

With his receding gray hair and salt-and-pepper mustache, Dr. Boch looks to be in his early fifties. He wears wire-rimmed glasses and gazes at the camera, his expression thoughtful. On the back of the photograph, he wrote, "To Margrieta in loyal friendship & deep gratitude for all the beauty given so graciously. All the best wishes for the future, January 1948."

Decades later, my mother added to Dr. Boch's inscription, "I was always proud of this statement." He gave her a vision of herself to which she would return.

When I first read Dr. Boch's words and before I understood their relationship, I assumed he was my mother's lover and that the "beauty given so graciously" had a sexual implication. Only later did I recognize that Dr. Boch meant more than physical beauty. He was talking about a loveliness of spirit—an inner radiance—something my mother possessed, though I rarely experienced it. Other people, other people's children, saw that light and felt its warmth.

Whenever my mother spoke of Vienna, long after she had departed, I had the feeling she was conjuring some mythical place that held a meaning for her I did not understand. Even the way she said the word—*Veerna*, the sound drawn out, probably her pronunciation of Wien, "Vienna" in German—made the city and her history there feel separate. It was something she held back, and as an adolescent, I resented it. It was as though that had been her real life and the one she lived with us the imitation.

I understand my mother's six years in Austria differently now. When she recalled Vienna, it wasn't so much to reject the life we lived but to remind herself of who she had been, a woman not only ambitious for happiness but one who believed in the promise of its realization.

Maternal Instincts

My grandmother and mother both stand in profile in the photograph. My mother reaches to place her left hand just above Lee's right elbow, while Lee extends her right arm to cradle my mother's left. Lee looks toward the camera, a coquettish smile on her face in which I find little to suggest the maternal. My mother, in turn, gazes up at Lee, but she doesn't smile or lean her body against her mother's. Were I to guess at her thoughts, I would say that she wanted to project whatever would most please Lee—in this case, a vision of filial devotion. But I knew my grandmother. And I have my mother's stories.

We called her Lee, though that wasn't her name. I started it as a small child because I could not pronounce Lydia. The notion that we might call her Granny, Gram, Nana, or any of the other names children give their grandmothers was quickly discarded.

When Lee arrived in the United States in 1949, she lied about her age to make herself younger, and as she looked the part, she got away with it. Strangers sometimes mistook her for my mother, and even as a small child, I knew she enjoyed the illusion. Years later, after her appearance had started to catch up with her actual age, she wore a blonde wig over her thinning hair. Under the wig's edge, I could see the ends of the Band-Aids she had placed on the sides of her ears to pull the skin taut. A do-it-yourself facelift.

For a few years, Lee lived in the front bedroom on the third floor of our Pine Street house in West Philadelphia. My grandfather Paul occupied the room next to hers, and my sister and I the back bedroom on the other side of the stairs and next to the only bathroom. Lee and Paul ignored each other, as their private war had ended, though without either side victorious.

One afternoon, while I was at school, in first or second grade, Lee took my box of Crayola crayons, sixty-four with a built-in sharpener. I'd never seen so many colors, more than ten shades of blue alone—turquoise to midnight to blue violet. The crayons had names like *cadet blue*, *spring green*, and *bittersweet*. I tried to keep them in perfect condition, never pushing down too hard as I drew trim houses with curtains on the windows and apple trees in the front yards, a big yellow sun.

She gave the box to my brother Billy, who didn't possess the dexterity to handle the crayons without damaging them. When I returned home, I found him scribbling lopsided circles on white paper. A couple of broken crayons lay next to him. Perhaps I only yelled at him, but I might have pushed him too, snatched his drawing away. He might have cried.

In response to my outburst, Lee grabbed the orange box and broke all the remaining crayons one by one, screaming at me while she did it. I can still hear her strident voice, the sharp snap of each crayon, both sounds obliterating even the thought of protest. Transfixed by her fury, Billy and I could not move.

My brother and I did not talk about the incident until decades later, and then, only by chance. He remembers that he both wanted and didn't want to play with the crayons. The bright colors attracted him, but he knew he shouldn't touch them and wouldn't have if Lee had not pressed the crayons upon him. When he watched our grandmother destroy something he understood I treasured, he believed it was his fault and that I would never forgive him.

I suspect he felt that way for some time, and that fear affected our relationship as children, like a splinter of glass that makes its way under the skin.

A memory fragment stays with me but never coalesces into scene. I am quite young, perhaps in third grade. I am on my knees in front of the low coffee table in our living room, on which sits an electric keyboard. Several adults are in the room, my father among them, but he isn't paying attention to me. I have been encouraged to play something. I cannot remember ever learning anything on this instrument, but I must have, because I play some simple melody. Afterward, the adult conversation continues, and I probably wander away.

But here's what I do remember. Shortly thereafter, Lee offered my father's inattentiveness as proof that he had no interest in me. She did not go so far as to tell me that he did not love me, but I heard the hint, and could draw my own conclusions.

In *Lost in Transmission: Studies of Trauma Across Generations*, contributors examine the ways in which traumatic experience cut off from social discourse in one generation passes on to the next. Now, years later, without anyone to ask about my hypothesis, I wonder if Lee's interpretation of my father's behavior related to her own unspoken trauma. Was my grandmother's observation of my father's behavior connected to her own history? Was she warning me of the danger posed by a father's interest in his daughter?

The little I know of Lee's history comes from my mother, and she regretted not knowing more. In particular, my mother wondered about Lee's father and the reasons for his departure from the family home. He never returned, and when his wife, my great-grandmother, learned of her estranged husband's death, she said that now she could die, because he was gone. Perhaps she held to the memory of the man Peter had been before a traumatic brain injury changed him in intolerable ways.

An engineer, he had been organizing workers to form a trade union when he was attacked and severely beaten. His personality and behavior changed following the assault. He started abusing his daughters; my mother never learned the nature of the abuse but suspected it might have been sexual.

Lee and her sisters told their mother that unless their father left the family home, they would do so. My great-grandmother chose her daughters.

I find a collection of photographs in a spiral-bound set of plastic sleeves, the cover long gone. I recognize my grandmother with two older adolescent girls I take to be Marta and Alma, her sisters. Lee, the middle daughter, also had two younger sisters and one much younger brother. Another brother died in infancy.

In one photograph, Lee sits on the floor, peonies or roses in one hand, a mirror in the other. Alma sits in a chair, holding a piece of paper above the open book in her lap. Marta stands to the side, clutching a handkerchief in her right hand. No one smiles. They wear demure dark dresses with white collars; Lee's has lace edging. Her wavy hair looks bobbed, while Marta and Alma each have long hair gathered into single braids tied with elaborate ribbons, velvet. Lee's finer features and striking eyes—I know them to be a purplish blue—offer a glimpse of the beauty she will become.

Marta's arched brow and downturned mouth make her appear suspicious and disapproving. Alma's dark eyes look blank, as if she has withdrawn into disappointment. Lee's gaze conveys an uneasy watchfulness. I scan their faces, searching for narrative, but keep returning to the one I would impose based on what I know of their father. The timing fits, but more than that, the feeling the image evokes does as well. A feeling of loss.

Something else Lee said comes back to me, and now, I look for another meaning in her words. Not long before she departed Pine Street, she made a dress for me—cream-colored in a polyester fabric, an A-line design, and more flattering than anything else I had as a plump fifth grader. As she pinned the dress during a final fitting, one of her pins pricked my side, and I flinched. "You have to suffer to be beautiful," she said. I wonder now if her maxim actually meant that being beautiful means you *will* suffer.

I do not know how the task of evicting our grandmother fell to my sister and me. I see us, two little girls, standing before our grandmother, holding hands. I am older by sixteen months, but it's Lydia who speaks for us both: "Daddy won't come home unless you leave." My father had departed the house to stay at the hospital where he worked. Lydia remembers him telling her that he would not return as long as Lee lived at Pine Street; that would have been what pushed her into the room. I'm not sure about my own motivation. I like to think I wanted to protect my sister from having to face our grandmother alone, but it may be that I just wanted the constant tension Lee provoked between my parents to go away.

How could you have left that to us? I would like to ask my mother. She might tell me that she had tried to get her mother out of the house without success, and that's probably true. But her failure to act meant we had to take her place. If I could ask my father, he might say he *had* acted by leaving.

Lee divided us—my sister and my youngest brother, Henry, most often on one side; Billy and me on the other. Henry recently told me that he'd been golden when it came to our grandmother. In the world of our childhood, that meant someone else had to be dross.

After Lee had moved to an apartment, she would hang a white sheet from her window on the days she made lunch for Henry, then in third or fourth grade and attending the public school across the street. Absent the signal, Henry would meander home to Pine Street for bologna on white bread. A chef now, he still remembers Lee's meals—cabbage stuffed with ground pork and raisins, cold plates of meat and cheese, tart pickles and black bread, or his favorite, *piragi*, traditional Latvian buns filled with sautéed onion and smoked pork.

Lee sometimes told him she wished she still lived at Pine Street, that she would be there but for our parents.

I rarely visit Lee. I do not like going to her apartment alone, as that makes me too much of a target. But I'm older now—eleven or twelve—and Lydia is with me. From the apartment's windows I watch the wind push leaden clouds along the horizon, a storm threatening. Late afternoon in summer, the trees heavy with dark green leaves. The apartment smells of old wool and cooking oil.

The couch on which I sit may once have served as a twin bed. Lee has covered it with a Persian rug in a geometric pattern of cranberry, ivory, and black—rough against the backs of my legs. She has fashioned decorative pillows from scraps of embroidery but placed them too far back for comfort. On the wall hangs a faded tapestry in gold and brown, giving the room the feel of a distant place and time.

I chew the inside of my cheek, scratch idly at a mosquito bite, can't figure out what to do with my hands. In the next few minutes, I will say something to anger my grandmother, or perhaps it will be my silence that inflames her. Whatever the spark, her next words are an ultimatum. Either I respond as she demands or leave her apartment. Without a jacket or umbrella, I have no protection against the rain and wind outside.

I get up and walk out the door. Though nervous, I feel determined. I will not be cowed by her, even if that means walking back to Pine Street alone in the thunderstorm.

Christmas around this same time. I stand in our living room, our fir tree in the corner. We decorated it the night before with glass balls—red, silver, gold, green, a few blue ones, my favorites for their scarcity—tinsel clumped in spots where we grew sloppy toward the end, and multicolored lights. The scent of roasting turkey blends with the tang of evergreen. A cloudy mid-afternoon, damp from a recent rain, not overly cold. The light from the room's large windows soft, as if filtered through muslin.

I open the door to Lee, having seen her approach through the living room window. She probably has a few packages with her, as she would not have come empty-handed. My sister and brothers must have also seen our grandmother, because I am suddenly alone. I can hear their retreating steps as they scatter to other parts of the house. My father isn't home yet, perhaps still at the hospital checking on patients. My mother stays in the kitchen, though she probably heard her mother's arrival.

Lee wears makeup and a colorful dress in some shiny fabric, something she has sewn, as she is a skilled seamstress. My stomach flutters, as it often does in her presence. I do not know how to talk to her. I am grateful when she goes to the kitchen in search of my mother. She doesn't stay there long.

Returning to the living room, Lee picks up her coat, but doesn't put it on. She seems to be waiting for something. The silence pools around us. After a few minutes, she gives a brief nod, as if she's come to a decision. "Merry Christmas," she says, before leaving to walk back to her apartment. In that instant I know she had hoped my mother would invite her to stay.

It is the first time I ever feel sympathy for her.

That moment, so long ago now, haunts me, even though I had nothing to do with the erosion of my mother's relationship with my grandmother, a deterioration resulting from an accumulation of wounds, many of which I will never learn anything about. And yet, my mother and grandmother remained connected. It couldn't have been otherwise. Wars eventually end. The ties to your mother do not.

"For a very little child," my mother reminded me, "parents are like gods." When my mother still believed in the omnipotence of her parents, and especially her mother, Lee sometimes told her, "I gave you life and I can take it away." She possessed the temper to back up the threat. My mother told me of one beating that was so severe she could not go to school for several days. I did not question her further, but now I wonder about the circumstances. Was my mother physically unable to go to school, or did Lee keep her at home to avoid exposure? Visible bruises and welts would have challenged any illusion of familial harmony.

In another moment of rage, when my mother was already a young woman, Lee threw an iron at her face. The iron hit my mother on her right cheek, leaving a scar noted among "distinctive physical marks" on her June 1956 Certificate of Naturalization as an American citizen. Sometimes when I am ironing a pair of jeans or a cotton shirt, I consider the heft of the appliance in my hand and its potentially lethal destructiveness.

I attribute my grandmother's attack to jealousy over my mother's growing attractiveness to men, perhaps to a particular man in this instance, but that may be something I have imposed on the story. My mother came into beauty later than Lee, but she occupied that same territory.

One of the terrible ironies of trauma, M. Gerard Fromm notes in *Lost in Transmission*, is that the victimized may unconsciously attempt to reverse their traumatic helplessness by becoming victimizers themselves. Lee's cruelty toward my mother might have been her distorted way of confronting her own abuse.

A pudgy four-year-old, my mother looks nothing like Lee, whose beauty is so celebrated that her profile served as the model for an image on a Latvian coin. They are eating breakfast—strong coffee, rye bread and cheese, sweet butter. My mother has hot milk with chicory and honey, coffee for a child.

Paul reads the paper, oblivious to his surroundings, until Lee's voice makes him look up. "Am I not the most beautiful woman?" She's done her hair differently this morning, or perhaps it's the new blouse she's wearing; in any case, she is eager for the expected compliment.

Paul laughs and teases her that she looks like a shriveled mushroom.

My mother, hearing her father's mirth, mistakes what has just happened as a pleasantry between her parents. She joins in the apparent merriment but stops when she sees her mother isn't smiling.

Paul, still chuckling, collects his briefcase and hat, kisses his wife's cheek, and exits the apartment. Silence fills the kitchen, and my mother senses something is wrong. Lee turns to her and says that because she laughed, she must leave. She picks up the cup of hot milk, removes the plate on which rests a half-eaten piece of buttered bread, and puts them in the sink. She goes into my mother's room and picks out some clothes, puts them in a basket. From the kitchen, she adds a piece of fruit, a slice of bread. She grips my mother's arm and forces her from the chair, leads her toward the door. She opens the door and tells her to go, her hand firm on my mother's back, pushing her forward.

My mother doesn't know where to go, but understands she has to do as her mother has commanded. She starts walking down the stairs, her basket knocking on each step. Lee lets her go, calling her back only when she sees that her ruse has worked. She tells her it was only a joke.

Looking back, I realize that my grandmother repeated a variation of her cruel prank with me, and though the result was the same—my mother and I were both cast out—I was much older, and my response differed. My mother departed the apartment because she believed she had no choice but to obey Lee, on whom she was wholly dependent. I left my grandmother's presence out of defiance.

My mother always insisted my grandfather was a good father, but I find that credible only in contrast to Lee's parenting. When I pressed her for examples of her father's loving care, she described how he would place her on his shoulders and walk around his office while she pointed to the busts of famous philosophers, identifying them by name. At a very young age, she could quote Immanuel Kant's maxims in German, especially those with a singsong quality: "*Die Wissenschaft ist organisiertes Wissen. Weisheit ist organisiertes Leben*," which translates to "Science is organized knowledge. Wisdom is organized life."

"He thought I was so smart," she said.

At that age, my mother couldn't understand any aspect of Kant's philosophy, but she had learned how to perform for her father.

"He catered to me," my mother continued. He took her for walks, just the two of them, slowing his pace to accommodate her small steps. Sometimes they went to the large park near their Riga apartment. In winter's clear cold, the snow a carpet over withered grass, he pulled her sled, as she toddled next to him holding his hand.

In my favorite photograph of my mother and her father, they stand in a courtyard. My mother, age seven or eight, wears a short-sleeved cotton dress, her father a suit, so the weather must have been temperate. He is turned slightly to the right, his left shoulder against a tree, so that we see his face at an angle. He looks to the side, a bemused smile on his face. His spread palm on my mother's chest holds her close. She grins as she tilts her head back against her father's torso, leaning into him. It's the leaning in that captures my attention.

I felt the same comfort when I first knew my grandfather. He lived with us from the time I was a toddler until his death when I was fifteen. My mother said he was a great help to her, taking care of us while she worked. I've seen photographs of him holding my sister's and my hands on the sidewalk in front of our house—two little girls of four and five in red and black tights, fitted coats and wool hats, tiny handbags over our arms—vamping for the camera.

I learned the multiplication table to please him. While he sat in the glider on our porch and smoked his pipe, I'd walk back and forth reciting the numbers to 10 times 10. Perhaps he thought I was smart too. I waited to clean his pipe, believing myself chosen for the task. He'd hand it to me, and I'd carry it carefully to the brick walkway in front of the house, tapping it gently on the ground to empty out the tobacco. I would have done anything for him then.

But our relationship didn't survive my brother's birth. Or, at least, that's how it felt to me. I remember going to his room on the house's third floor. I stood at the threshold, hoping to join my little brother and him. Billy was about two, so I would have been six. "Go away," he said, "I have Billy now." And I did go away.

I see a similarity between my experience and my mother's past. Neither of us felt chosen by those we loved. "I remember all my childhood," she told me, "I was always filled with some kind of fear that my parents might get rid of me." She even identified her replacement—the daughter of a senior administrator at her father's college. Ilga was a year younger and a "very obedient child," my mother said, "in a very nice family." My mother, though obedient too, was frequently admonished to be more like Ilga.

She would watch the slender blonde girl, so much daintier than she, and wonder how she might transform herself. She could be quieter, more respectful. She could keep her clothes cleaner, her hair combed, stand up straighter. She could take up less space. She could make her parents happier. Then her parents would stop fighting. Then they might be like Ilga's parents. Then she might breathe.

My mother characterized her father as "a really horrible husband, really horrible as husbands go," but that did not compromise her love for him. She could separate his two roles. I could not do that when it came to my own father, but that may be because my relationship with him was impaired from the beginning. I didn't have enough memories of him as attentive and nurturing to mitigate my observations of him as a husband.

Paul was established professionally and some ten years older than Lee when they met at Latvia's Interior Ministry, where he held a senior position and she worked as a secretary. Educated and successful, attractive, if not quite handsome, Paul was a desirable husband. Lee's family respected him. "After all," my mother said, "he was a big guy."

My grandmother, in her early twenties, hesitated to accept Paul's marriage proposal. Latvia, newly independent from the Soviet Union, had only recently emerged from the First World War. Perhaps her country's freedom made my grandmother wish to explore her own, rather than accept the constraints imposed by marriage. Or, perhaps, something about my grandfather concerned her; in any case, it took Paul some time to persuade her.

Once married, whatever Lee's interests and desires, Paul expected her to sacrifice them to ensure his comfort. She created and maintained their beautiful apartment, acted as hostess, and took care of my mother, responsibilities likely mirrored by other married women of her social class. It's not her role as wife I find striking; it's my grandfather's complete disinterest in her as an individual.

Paul served on the board of directors of a major cruise line and could travel internationally on their vessels free of charge. He never took Lee with him, as her presence might have interfered with his own itinerary of visits to museums and concert halls. He didn't want to be bothered with activities that might please her.

"Lee never had a birthday party, but my father's birthdays were always grand affairs," my mother said, in another telling example of her father's self-absorption. Paul was a "supreme egoist," she said. She believed his character the result of both nature—he'd simply been born that way—and nurture. His mother, Anna, spoiled him as her oldest and only surviving child. His younger brother had died during the First World War. "Everything was for Pauli."

Anna never liked my grandmother, because Lee was not the bride she'd had in mind for her beloved son. When my grandfather defied his mother to marry Lee, he may have felt a particular claim on her devotion. He expected her to obey and follow his lead absolutely, and when she didn't, he erupted in anger.

My mother described these fits of temper as "grand slam scandals," during which her father smashed light fixtures with the heavy board he wielded, overturned tables. Later, in response to my direct question, she admitted that Paul had also abused Lee physically. Her disclosure surprised me, because it revealed a brutish side to my grandfather I'd not known existed and one my mother had never previously acknowledged.

It's after midnight and the guests have departed. With all the wine consumed at the party, Lee sleeps soundly. My mother, hypervigilant, has trouble settling next to her mother. She tenses at the noise of her father stomping about the apartment, his angry mumblings, the shattering of glass. Perhaps he thinks Lee flirted too much at the party or enjoyed too much another man's attention. In any case, he is jealous and that jealousy, as my mother knows, will lead to violence.

Suddenly, Paul pushes open the door to the bedroom. He strides to the bed and starts pulling off the bed linens. My mother and Lee, now fully awake, scramble from the bed. Lee demands he stop, while my mother stands rooted in place. Having torn blankets and sheets from the bed, he leaves the room, returning minutes later with a large bucket of water. He drenches the bed, tosses the bucket. It makes a hollow sound as it hits the floor. He starts moving toward Lee, his fists clenched, and my mother hurls herself at him, pushing him back, leaning in. She pleads with him to stop. Perhaps the physical exertion has sobered him, because he leaves the room.

Not long after this incident, my mother devised a kind of pulley system. It allowed her to close the door to the bedroom from a distance, though I doubt it prevented her father from entering if he were determined to do so. "Can you imagine, a nine-year-old doing such a thing?" she asked.

I can, because I understand a nine-year-old's fear. I was only a couple of years older when I started to dread being together with my parents, because of the anxiety I felt around them. I waited for the destruction to begin, not necessarily of a physical nature, but dangerous in a different way. Their marriage had started to implode, and that disintegration left me without any secure place to stand.

Summers offered my mother escape from her parents' combat. From about age six until age thirteen, as school ended in early June, she left Riga for her paternal grandparents' home in Valka, a small town in the north of Latvia. Surrounded by farms and forests—of Scottish pine and Norway spruce, silver birches—Valka rested on one side of the winding Pedele River. Its twin, Valga, occupied the opposite shore in Estonia, the two towns within walking distance.

She did not miss her parents during these months away. As she departed each summer, she would plead with them to remain calm and not to hurt each other, and then, I like to think, she thought no more about them.

I have a photograph of my mother with her paternal grandparents, Jakob and Anna, the bright sun making them all squint as they look toward the camera. Anna and Jakob sit close to each other, Anna's arm draped over her husband's leg. My young mother, already brown from sunny days outside, stands behind them, her thin arms wrapped around her grandmother's neck, a contented smile on her face. Gone is the watchfulness in my mother's gaze and carriage, so apparent in photographs of her with her parents.

In another photograph, my mother sits on Jakob's lap. She's six or seven and may have just finished swimming, as her legs and torso are bare. Sunlight filters through what looks to be a holly tree behind her, dappling her face and shoulders. Jakob and my mother wear wide grins, as though responding to a shared joke.

Jakob and Anna's spacious apartment likely included a room for my mother, kept ready in anticipation of her visits. At night she nestles in a feather bed, her light quilt warm against her skin. Next to the bed stands a small walnut table with a glass lamp. On the table, a bird's feather and a smooth grayish-white stone, treasures found earlier on walks with her grandparents. Against the far wall, her wardrobe, filled with her summer clothes. A casement window overlooks the apartment's large garden, where my mother played hide-and-seek with the neighbor's children. On rainy days they shared the games and toys Jakob and Anna had acquired to satisfy the whims of their only grandchild. Other days, my mother visited the farm, only twelve miles away, owned by Jakob's brother and his family. When I was young, she bought me a toy farm. I loved the red-roofed barn made of tin and the tiny plastic animals—cows and chickens, horses, at least one dog.

I recognize an element of longing in my imagining of my mother's summers with Anna and Jakob, because I wish I'd had grandparents I loved and they me. My parents were both only children, so no aunts or uncles enriched my life. I had no one to counterbalance my parents' influence—no familial haven to which I could retreat in the face of my parents' discord—so that their effects on me were somehow magnified.

My mother once said that her father loved Lee like oxygen. "You can't live without air," she said, "but you don't recognize its existence." Paul did not notice Lee until she attracted the attention of other men.

When my mother was still a small child, six or so, her parents stopped sharing the same bedroom. By the time she was eight, she understood that her mother's romantic interests lay elsewhere, but that reality had to remain unacknowledged.

"Lee had lovers," my mother said, and "Paul was extremely jealous, but Lee was his wife and in the household. They attended all occasions together. It was sub-rosa."

My mother sits with her father reading in the study, political history for him, *The Life and Adventures of Robinson Crusoe* for her. The phone rings and she picks it up, knowing intuitively that it would be better if she, rather than her father, speak to the caller.

A gentleman's voice, one she's heard before, asks for her mother. Perhaps this gentleman is the Latvian military attaché, whose love affair with her mother will lead to a brief consideration of divorce, until her father uses his political influence to have the man transferred to Argentina.

My mother tells the caller that Lee has gone out shopping and that she will let her mother know of the call when she returns. Paul, who heard her response, asks who called. And now my young mother has a choice, but it's an easy one. It was Mrs. So-and-So, she tells him.

Years later, Lee will tell my mother how touched she had been by her efforts to protect her. And my mother will realize that Lee hadn't understood her motivation at all. She didn't lie to shield Lee; she lied to protect herself by preserving her family's fragile peace.

For several years, starting when my mother was in grade school, my grandmother attended Riga's English Institute, and upon graduation became a teacher of English and English literature; eventually, she taught Russian as well. Her increased financial independence empowered her to follow her own desires. The war, when it began, may also have played a role; the threats under which she lived emboldened her. At the same time, they served to moderate my grandfather's response to her infidelity. Perhaps in the context of the loss of his country, the destruction of his marriage seemed like collateral damage. Or, perhaps, Paul simply grew tired of fighting with Lee.

In late summer of 1941, as Germany solidified its control over Latvia, my grandmother started a romance with a highly ranked German officer, a man she met at a party given by a close family friend. A Latvian and descendant of the Baltic German nobility, Frederick had returned to Riga with the German forces. He may have been grateful to find himself in his native country once again, despite the circumstances. I want to believe he opposed Hitler, if only privately, because of my grandmother's and mother's feelings for him, and also, because he ultimately abandoned his responsibilities as a German officer.

My mother would have been eighteen that summer, and perhaps for the first time had started to empathize with her mother, at least when it came to her affairs. "I was glad Lee loved Frederick," my mother said. "He was a wonderful man, an aristocrat in spirit."

My grandfather, aware of the relationship's intensity, decided to meet with Frederick. He asked him to come to his offices at the college. I imagine the scene.

Paul notices the German officer's carriage—his erect posture and physical grace. He rises from his chair and extends his hand across the desk. Frederick removes his cap, places it under his arm, and reaches to clasp my grandfather's hand. They nod to each other. Paul invites Frederick to sit, and they move to the leather sofa in front of the fireplace, as if this meeting were a polite encounter between two colleagues. They respect each other and regret finding themselves in opposition. Under different circumstances they might have been friends.

Paul offers Frederick some refreshment—coffee or tea. The office smells of leather and pipe tobacco. Afternoon light spills over the Persian carpet, the ornate clock on the bookshelf behind the desk marks the time, the sound a steady heartbeat.

Both men know why they are here but wish to preserve a minute or two of conviviality before moving beyond the pleasantries. My grandfather begins with a question, one to which he knows the answer, but wishes to have Frederick's confirmation. *You are a married man . . . involved with my wife?*

Frederick explains that he is in love with Lee and intends to divorce his wife. *I would like to marry her.* His words hang between them.

My grandfather recognizes that he possesses little power over this German officer, other than an appeal to his character. But he does not want to appear weak; neither man will accept the role of supplicant. If Lee's desire to leave him causes him pain, he does not reveal his suffering.

Paul is not sure how he will respond until he speaks the words. *I will give freedom to my wife, but you must give me your word of honor as an officer that you will not see her until you are divorced.*

Frederick gives his word of honor and then returns to his apartment, where he places his Luger in his mouth and pulls the trigger.

Lee's key fits smoothly in the lock as she turns it and opens the door to Frederick's apartment. She calls out a greeting, though she doesn't expect to find him at home at this hour. She's brought flowers, late-blooming roses from an otherwise neglected garden. She goes into the kitchen, chooses a yellow ceramic pitcher from the cabinet, fills it with water. She takes her time, admiring the colors of the roses—ballet slipper pink to magenta, the delicate dark green leaves. The bouquet will add a splash of color in the living room, a surprise for Frederick when he returns in the early evening.

That's where she finds him. He's sitting in an upholstered chair, his head thrown back, his face toward the ceiling. She notices the blue-black pistol on the carpet beside him.

She says his name, pleading. *Frederick.*

I doubt my grandfather anticipated Frederick's suicide. According to my mother, Lee did not blame him for Frederick's death, even though Paul's bargain with the German officer had set it in motion. My grandfather may have believed Frederick would withdraw, and in his absence, Lee might return to him.

Frederick survived in the hospital for a week, conscious and lucid for some of that time. His lucidity likely saved Lee's life, because he was able to make a statement on her behalf.

The German military authorities viewed Frederick's suicide attempt during wartime as treason, suicide being a betrayal of his duty as a German officer. Investigators hypothesized that my grandmother was a Soviet spy who had somehow forced Frederick's hand. Frederick absolved Lee of any responsibility, and the investigation ended.

My mother visited Frederick as he lay dying. The frontal bone of his skull had been removed, but his eyes remained an unclouded blue gray. She sat next to his bed and held his hand. *I love you*, she told him, realizing it was true. And her feelings for him didn't diminish those for her father; Frederick and Paul were alike in some ways, both dreamers, if different kinds. Maybe what she loved about Frederick was how he had affected her mother.

Frederick's affair with Lee had been going on for about eight months when he killed himself. His thoughts before he pulled the trigger are unknowable and the extremity of his act shocking. It may be that some deep melancholy plagued him before he met my grandmother, and she had been the antidote. He may have recognized that divorce was not feasible, or, if possible, not during wartime. Distaste with the role he had been called to play for Nazi Germany may have increased his despair. He did not wish to face the void Lee's absence would create in his life. Without her, he no longer saw a future that drew him forward. Suicide, in that moment of profound hopelessness, offered Frederick escape.

"That's the German officers' code of honor," my mother said. "It would have been inconceivable for him to break his word. They are not pragmatists like Americans are, who would use common sense." Frederick may have resolved to kill himself when he committed to relinquishing Lee.

I do not remember when I first heard the story of Frederick's suicide, but I knew of it as a teenager. His death added a note of high drama, romance even, to my mother's recollections of the war. In my mother's account, Lee became a secondary character, whose role served to reveal the resolve of this German officer. And yet, I wonder at the effect his death had on my grandmother. What vision of the future did Frederick's suicide destroy? Was her grief tinged with anger that Frederick's personal honor ultimately meant more to him than she? Did some sliver of pride exist for what love for her could inspire?

Lee met Rudi, the Austrian officer in the Wehrmacht with whom she fell in love, after Frederick's suicide. "I liked him very much," my mother said. "He was a man of energy, of enterprise, and one of the handsomest men I knew, like a better-looking Julius Caesar."

Rudi facilitated Lee and my mother's escape to Vienna, and once the war ended he joined my grandmother there. They moved to a farm estate in the countryside, where they served as co-managers, while my mother stayed in Vienna. The farm stood deep in the Soviet occupation zone.

One afternoon, after a visit, Lee is taking my mother back to the ferry that will traverse the Danube and return her to her apartment in the city. She drives a horse-drawn carriage, the reins loose in her hands, her voice seductive as she encourages the horses. My mother sits beside her, with space for passengers behind them. It is late summer or early fall, the weather still temperate, the birches beginning their turn toward gold. They travel along smoothly, listening to the rhythm of the horses trotting on the dirt road, the occasional trill of a bird in the woods.

Before they left the estate, Lee had warned my mother not to speak Russian if they were stopped. "Pretend you don't understand and remain silent," she said. Russian soldiers were scouring the woods for remnants of General Vlasov's regiment, along with loyalists who might have sheltered them. A decorated Soviet officer, Vlasov had been captured by the Germans during the siege of Leningrad. While a prisoner of war, he switched sides to fight for the Third Reich, believing—I assume—that Stalin posed the greater threat to his homeland. As my mother and grandmother believed the same, they would have had at least some sympathy for the general.

Ahead of them and just off the road, a Russian soldier stands among the trees. He raises one arm, signaling for them to stop. Lee and my mother exchange glances. Lee smiles, shrugs, gestures to the seat behind them. The soldier lumbers into the wagon. Without a word, Lee urges the horses forward.

Minutes pass. Then—*bang!*—the soldier fires his revolver between my mother's and Lee's heads.

Lee, "mad as a hornet," my mother said later, forgets that she doesn't speak Russian. She whips her head around and starts swearing at the soldier—a string of "unbelievably colorful" Russian curses, each one maligning generations of the soldier's family.

The soldier snarls, "Ah, you are with Vlasov, and I will report you."

My mother sits mute with fear. She understands the consequences of falling into Soviet hands. But Lee refuses to be intimidated. She replies with a threat of her own. "Vlasov? I am General Zhukov's lover, and he will have you shot in the morning." Zhukov, the most successful Russian general of the war, was known as the man who did not lose a battle. The same might be said of my grandmother.

The soldier apologizes, saying he'd only fired the revolver for fun, just to see what they'd do. Last time he did it, he said, the Austrians ran into the woods, and it took him all morning to find them.

My mother told me this story in admiration of Lee's daring and what she described as her physical courage. "One of her fine moments," she said. I doubt she ever shared that assessment with Lee.

"You didn't see the best of Lee," my mother said, which is why, like my mother, I cherish this anecdote. My grievances with my grandmother outweighed whatever I might have admired. She was my grandmother—not someone I could consider objectively—and, from my perspective, my mother's nemesis.

I only came to appreciate Lee's strength and determination after her death. She immigrated to the United States with few belongings and meager savings. Once here, she worked for modest wages, first as a secretary at Westinghouse Electric and then as a seamstress for Nan Duskin, a luxury women's clothing store in downtown Philadelphia.

After she died, my brothers, my sister, and I each received bequests of $12,500. That unexpected gift provided the down payment on Tom's and my first house. Lee saved our inheritance through hard work, and by denying herself whatever small luxuries might have sweetened her life. I cannot say what they would have been; I didn't know her well enough. But she lived in small apartments, never went anywhere on vacation, did not entertain, and limited her spending to the essentials of housing and food.

Not long after the incident with the Russian soldier, Lee was forced to flee the estate to escape interrogation and probable arrest by the Soviets as an "enemy of the state." Rudi's ex-wife, jealous of the woman she viewed as responsible for her divorce, informed the Soviet authorities that my grandmother was Latvian, not Austrian, as her identity papers claimed.

"Well, that was an act of hatred," I commented when my mother told me this story. She agreed but went on to say that she understood the woman's hatred, because Lee had taken her husband away.

"She didn't know Lee. She was mad that her husband had divorced her. She didn't even have to think about the real consequences. All she wanted was to get Lee away from there, which she did."

My grandmother returned to Vienna, rented an apartment, and hoped to maintain her freedom. Separated from her lover, she began finding fault with him, small grievances that nevertheless undermined the relationship. Perhaps Lee held Rudi responsible for his ex-wife's behavior, or perhaps, as my mother suggested, some vestige of loyalty to my grandfather prevented her from committing fully to another man. In any case, my mother didn't blame Rudi for the affair's end. "It wasn't Rudi's fault," my mother said. "Rudi was a great guy."

My mother, who rarely expressed remorse for opportunities missed, told me that she wished Lee had married Rudi. "It was a big mistake that she didn't. She would have lived a much better life here if she'd had Rudi. He would have established some kind of status for himself in the United States."

Lee never divorced Paul, though they did not live together again as husband and wife.

⚜ ⚜ ⚜

I asked my mother how her parents' marriage had affected her, and she told me that she had felt "somehow soiled by [her] household," and that she had been determined "to be truthful to a husband." Unlike my father, my mother remained faithful throughout her marriage, though I would not equate faithfulness with emotional engagement.

In the face of my father's infidelity, as a teenager, I once urged my mother to have an affair. My presumption appalls me now, though my mother never commented on it. At the time, I believed myself to be angrier than she about my father's extramarital relationship, one he made no effort to conceal. I am not sure what I hoped an affair would achieve, but I wanted to see my mother take some kind of action. That may be why I look at my grandmother's infidelity and feel the urge to cheer her on. I see a woman bound to a self-absorbed and sometimes abusive man, a woman who reached elsewhere for happiness. But I am looking at her as a woman with emotional and physical desires that had nothing to do with her role as a mother. At the same time, I recognize that my grandmother's affairs had consequences for her daughter. As a child, my mother had to be complicit with Lee, or risk being swept away by her father's rage.

Nancy Friday, in her book *My Mother/My Self*, acknowledges that maternal instinct has as many meanings as there are scientists, and that a significant number of these experts argue that it is a myth. In any case, she asserts, a mother's love does not emerge automatically as a result of her child's birth. The day-to-day caring for her child creates the relationship.

One of the last stories my mother told me about Lee involved the circumstances of my mother's birth, and so I can envision the scene.

A day in mid-winter. My grandmother, pregnant with my mother, is organizing a dinner party for Paul's visiting cousin when she goes into a complicated and difficult labor. When my grandfather arrives home, no doubt anticipating the linen-draped table, fresh flowers and polished cutlery, savory aromas emanating from the kitchen, he finds Lee in bed and in terrible distress. Rather than expressing compassion and concern for her, he fumes about the aborted dinner party. He eventually calls the doctor but refuses to do anything more to help. At some point, the doctor, outraged by my grandfather's tirade, admonishes him that his wife might die in childbirth, and that under the circumstances, he should stop criticizing.

My mother remembered this story, one Lee must have told her, as an example of her father's boorish behavior. It is undeniably that, but, in retrospect, I think it is more. It is a story of childbirth-related trauma.

Not every woman who survives such an experience emerges traumatized, but my grandmother may have been more vulnerable to lasting damage, not only because of Paul's failure to support her during the crisis but because of injuries sustained earlier in her life.

The difficult birth may have adversely affected the nascent bond between my grandmother and my mother and compromised their future relationship. At a minimum, Lee may have been physically unable to care for my mother until she, herself, recovered, and that would have put additional stress on them both.

Not long before my mother died, she told me that she had come to understand many things about Lee and that she had forgiven her many things. She forgave Lee for the physical abuse, believing she had been the scapegoat for her mother's ire at Paul. But she could not forgive the psychological torment. The threat of abandonment haunted her for a long time, perhaps always.

Marital strife might have fueled Lee's rage, but I believe its origins were older and more complicated. The horrors of the First World War, parental abuse, and other untold-of harm marked my grandmother. Her own history had been so infused with violence that she could not write a different one for my mother.

My Shadow Brother

I learn of my mother's abortions through a Connecticut weekly.

My sister-in-law, a reporter for the paper, wrote the article to commemorate the thirty-first anniversary of *Roe v. Wade*. She based the story on interviews she had conducted with several women willing to discuss their experiences, including my then-eighty-one-year-old mother.

The title screams, "I Had an Abortion." My jaws clench. A wave of exhaustion threatens my concentration. I consider retreating into sleep.

My mother had four abortions: three in Vienna during the Second World War and its aftermath, and a fourth in Philadelphia in 1952, after she had settled there. Four sounds like a lot. Four times my mother chose not to be a mother.

She explains that she initially disclosed her abortion history in response to a routine medical questionnaire. "When I broke my leg, I had to announce what surgeries I'd had, and I wrote them all down. If someone wants to think I'm a sinful bitch, I don't give a damn."

Sinful doesn't resonate with me—I do not view my mother's abortions as sin. *Bitch* hits home, though, because of what I read as her callousness. I exhale slowly. My feelings a closed fist.

My sister-in-law knew all the women she interviewed personally, and some, like her great-aunt and cousin, intimately, but still my mother stands out—as both a doctor and a woman, as a Latvian and an American citizen, as someone exceptionally candid. More tolerant attitudes prevailed in the Austria my mother knew. "You didn't have to keep it like a deadly secret. It was your private business. It was wartime, for Christ's sake."

The reference to her private business grated. If she had wanted to keep her abortions private, why tell a reporter, even if that reporter was her daughter-in-law?

Though not treated as a crime in Vienna, abortions carried other risks. As a medical student my mother had access to medical expertise, but not to anesthesia and antibiotics because they were not readily available.

One of her abortions turned septic; some of the placenta had remained in her uterus. "I bled and bled and bled and bled. I had an extremely high fever and bone-wracking chills. The thing is you get euphoric. I was in bed and thinking of the old Romans who would get into the bathtub and open their veins."

She had a convulsion, prompting her roommate to search Vienna for medical help. "She got a professor of gynecology, who was my lover too, and she hustled him over—he was not the father. He induced the placenta, and when I delivered the placenta, the bleeding stopped."

I quit reading then—or perhaps I continued on—but I'd lost my focus beyond the line "a professor of gynecology, who was my lover too. He was not the father."

I did not talk to my mother about her interview, not until years later. I buried both the article and my questions in the rigid container created by my judgment.

⚜ ⚜ ⚜

Looking back on my anger now, I search for its sources.

I read my mother's interview for the first time at age fifty, well past childbearing age, but not beyond the feelings of loss for the child Tom and I wanted but could not have. That said, and though it would have been understandable, my own infertility did not, as far as I know, affect my response to my mother's comments. I had hoped for a baby with Tom. My mother had not wanted a child. Both choices are legitimate. Her decision did not magnify my own regret.

Resentment that she had shared such personal information with my sister-in-law before telling me could have influenced my reading. My sister-in-law had posed the questions about abortion, and my mother provided the answers. At the same time, I wished my mother had kept the information to herself. Or, at a minimum, spoken to me before the article appeared, instead of letting me learn of her abortions as might a stranger.

Though I did not condemn my mother for having had abortions, four struck me as excessive. It seemed she had chosen abortion as a drastic form of contraception.

My anger came from what I perceived as my mother's complete lack of feeling, made starker by the comments of the other women interviewed. While acknowledging their gratitude that abortion had been available to them, they also spoke about the emotional complexities involved in making and living with that choice. My mother's account contained none of that sensitivity.

What I read as my mother's cavalier response to abortion made me feel implicated as her daughter, as though I might be called to explain or excuse her behavior. I hoped no one I knew would read the piece. I felt embarrassed.

The subject of abortion waits for my mother and me, for six years, until I more or less stumble upon it as a result of a book

I find on recording family histories. Our late 2010 discussion is the first of the final group of interviews I conducted with my mother, who by that time was living in Massachusetts.

Mid-morning, hours when my mother usually has more energy. She sits in Concord, and I sit several states away in Pittsburgh. Her voice sounds raw. She coughs and I wait for her to recover before posing my question. Years of smoking have robbed her of what had sounded like a cello's low song. That change reminds me that I am running out of time.

I ask her about her thoughts on abortion and she surprises me by returning to the environment she had encountered in the 1950s after her arrival in the United States, some of which she had addressed in the interview with my sister-in-law. "There was no talk. It was against the law, and you were prosecuted if you had evidence of an illegal abortion." As a doctor, she helped treat women who had undergone botched procedures—women traumatized first by what was frequently a catastrophic medical outcome and subsequently by law enforcement's responses.

In contrast, her abortions in Vienna were performed by doctors at home. Despite that expertise, her third abortion resulted in life-threatening complications.

I picture my mother lying gravely ill in the drafty apartment she shares with her roommate, Marga. It is frigid winter, and the apartment has no heat. A place of high ceilings and tall windows, worn wooden floors, rooms imbued with a barren elegance. She huddles in bed under a Persian rug, recently dragged from the floor, its once vibrant reds now faded. The weight creates a temporary illusion of warmth, but the dusty, rough carpet fails to stop her trembling. When her fevers return, she casts the rug aside, and for a moment, she feels free.

The pain that had gripped her abdomen has receded, or perhaps she's only grown accustomed to it. Her body so weakened by the loss of blood she feels hollow inside. She thinks she is going to die. She will not finish medical school, nor go to the United States, nor marry the Southerner a fortune teller had predicted for her long ago.

My mother might have died then, and I would never have been born, gone before she could even form an idea of me.

The professor of gynecology Marga called managed to stop the bleeding, but he didn't address the infection. "He didn't do anything whatsoever," my mother said.

"Why not?" I asked.

"I don't know. It was before penicillin. There wasn't much he could do." Penicillin had been discovered by then, but it wasn't available in postwar Vienna.

The doctor's response disturbs me. Had he already seen so much suffering in the war, that my mother's death would be merely one more to add to the ledger? Or perhaps his unresponsiveness resulted from a personal history he and my mother shared.

The infection eventually subsided, and my mother gradually recovered. Marga, who had access to a well-stocked American officers' club in Vienna, brought hot dogs home to her day after day, the protein critical to regaining her strength.

My mother imposed an emotional hierarchy on her abortions, one that placed the three in Vienna in one category and the fourth in another. Her pregnancies in Vienna occurred when contraception was not available—something I had not considered when I read her interview the first time—and with men she described as casual lovers: "I didn't intend to marry the father, and I certainly didn't want any child by him and not in wartime." She assured me that once she had terminated these pregnancies, she thought no more about them. I believe her, though I wonder if the abortions had a cumulative effect. Did each one deaden her to the next, so that the fourth was made possible by those that preceded it?

"The only abortion that I sometimes regretted . . . my future husband's baby, whom I intended to marry later, and did marry."

Until this conversation, I had not understood that my mother's fourth abortion involved a baby conceived with my father. I also hadn't grasped that my father had assisted my mother in terminating the pregnancy. The article stated this. I had read the words but had not absorbed their meaning.

"Do you mind talking about this?" I asked.

"Well, I was very upset that it appeared in the article, you know. Because I didn't think my name would be mentioned, that Daddy's name would be mentioned."

At the time of my sister-in-law's interview, my mother lived in a socially conservative Texas town; George W. Bush was president. President Bush's anti-abortion stance infuriated her, especially its roots in evangelical Christianity and what she saw as the latter's attempts to subjugate women's rights to control their own bodies. "It's usually the men who decide it," she said, "and evangelicals." Outrage prompted my mother to reveal her abortion history to my sister-in-law, and her anger likely blinded her to the consequences of participating in the interview.

I keep returning to the recording I made of my discussion with my mother. I've already transcribed our conversation, but am concerned I missed something, some nuance. I fidget in my chair, and when I get to the passages describing my mother's fourth abortion, a story I now know by heart, I start grinding my teeth. I notice how my voice falters, how I stumble over my questions. "I guess I'm meaning because . . . I want to go back in time a little bit . . . What, what . . . ?"

I try to explore the moment she discovers she's pregnant with my father's child, that interval between knowing and deciding. I look for hesitation, some emotional struggle over her response to this pregnancy, whose circumstances differ so from those she encountered in Vienna. Abortion then seemed like the only sane choice, but not in this instance. I want her to tell me she had doubts, that she thought about having this baby, that abortion—something that would require my father's active participation—was a fraught choice. I want her to be different, not the woman who turned away from the possibility of this child without considering the alternative. I want to warn her that her choice to terminate this pregnancy will have repercussions that will reverberate in ways she cannot anticipate—for her, in her marriage, and for me.

As for my father's reaction, I know nothing of his deliberations or feelings, except what my mother told me. He said he would marry her and have the child.

I have a photograph of him from his medical school yearbook taken around that time. He wears a tan jacket, a white shirt, and a striped tie. His unlined face reveals the faintest of creases at the corners of his mouth. I notice his strong nose, his dark eyes that narrow when he grins, though he does not smile in this photograph. His lips are full without being overly sensual. There is something both resolute and hopeful in his gaze. Perhaps these two qualities—confidence and optimism—pushed him toward wanting that baby.

It might be a summer afternoon. My parents find themselves free and want to leave the hospital, not worrying about a destination. The car's windows are down, green flashes on either side as they travel a tree-lined road. The air entering the car feels fresh. Summer's humidity, typical of Philadelphia, has yet to arrive.

My father hums "When Johnny Comes Marching Home," the Civil War song celebrating a soldier's triumphant return, and one of his favorite melodies. When he gets to "Hurrah, hurrah!" he sings the words and taps the steering wheel in time. He can't help himself. He feels invincible. He is graduating from one of the top medical schools in the country, despite his mother's admonition to be satisfied with an engineering degree and not aspire to more. And he's won this accomplished and beautiful woman sitting beside him. He'll marry her. He's sure.

My mother breathes deeply, hoping the clean air will calm her. She clenches and unclenches her hands in her lap. She's gone over what she needs to say, marshaled her arguments about this being her decision alone, about the timing being all wrong. She wants to get this over with, in the car, where she doesn't have to look in her future husband's eyes.

She fixes her gaze on the road ahead and announces, "I'm pregnant, but I am not going to have the baby."

My father turns toward her for an instant, a quickening in his chest. "Let's get married now," he says. What is there to think about? He loves her and she's pregnant with his child.

My mother told me once that she could never marry a man she could not envision as the father of her children. She expects to marry my father. She wants to have children with him—children are part of her life's plan—but she is not prepared to have this child at this time.

I return to the past looking for some argument my father might have made to change her mind, but I cannot find one. "Nobody is going to marry me because I am pregnant," she told him. "A matter of principle," she said. "No shotgun marriage."

I wonder whose judgment concerned her. My paternal grandmother, who never warmed to my mother, might have suggested that she had coerced my father into marriage by becoming pregnant. That criticism would have stung, even if my mother knew it lacked any foundation. There were others, too, who would have celebrated a perceived misstep—the nurses who resented her for being a doctor, for not being American. In the operating room, they would gossip, "We don't need displaced people here. Why should we be giving anything to her?"

She had arrived at the threshold of securing so much she had wanted—a career as a doctor, when she hadn't believed it would be possible in the United States, and marriage to a man she loved whose talent and ambition drew her to commit to a shared future. She believed an ill-timed pregnancy posed a threat.

My parents decide to meet in between their shifts at the hospital. When they find an empty procedure room, my father turns on the light, flooding the space in a harsh glare. The room smells of disinfectant. The walls are empty and painted a flat institutional white. Because the space must be ready for use, the exam table is already draped. My mother doesn't put on a hospital gown; she only removes her skirt and underpants. She lies on the metal table, bends her knees, places her heels in the metal footrests, eager for this to be over.

Would my father have numbed her cervix, or were they in too much of a hurry? They probably skipped this step. My mother had a high threshold for pain; the abortions she'd had in Vienna had proceeded without anesthesia. "They were very painful," she said, "but all right."

My father dilated my mother's cervix to induce premature labor and a miscarriage. His approach did not succeed. Over the course of several days, my mother bled some, but the pregnancy continued. Did reticence make my father less effective? Perhaps he could not make the transition from lover to trained clinician.

He may have felt relief, recognizing that he did not want the abortion. He had accommodated my mother because he believed the choice ultimately belonged to her. She would have sacrificed more—her professional aspirations, even something of her sense of self—had she proceeded with the pregnancy.

My father repeated his proposal that they marry and have the child, but my mother remained adamant. Even though unsuccessful and relatively benign, she feared their first attempt had damaged the embryo. When she did not miscarry, my parents agreed to make a second attempt. In the procedure room again, they arm themselves against feeling. This is a medical problem to be solved, nothing more or less. This is not the time to engage in any self-doubt. Proceeding requires this kind of single-mindedness.

My father performs both dilation and curettage, a procedure to remove tissue from inside my mother's uterus. And still, the pregnancy continues.

My mother wakes up every morning, her waist feeling thicker, her body sluggish. As her anxiety grows, she has trouble concentrating. She wants only one thing now: not to be pregnant.

Finally, at four months pregnant and alone in her apartment, my mother miscarried and delivered a dead fetus. She believed that the miscarriage resulted from the second attempt at abortion, despite the time that elapsed between the two events.

At sixteen weeks, a fetus weighs three to four ounces and is about four to five inches long, the skin is translucent, the skull is sufficiently developed that the eyes are positioned forward, faint eyelashes and brows are visible. Tiny bones in the ears are in place, making it likely that the fetus can hear his mother's voice in utero.

When she told my father, he asked, "What was it?"

"A boy."

"That's a shame," he responded, "because now you'll only have girls."

I do not know when in the pregnancy my parents made their second attempt at abortion, nor how much time passed between that procedure and the miscarriage. The longer I thought about this fourth abortion, the more I wanted answers to these questions. I hoped that by gathering all the details I would be able to construct a story that made sense to me. I believed information would give me greater control over my own reaction. *If I know exactly what happened*, I reasoned, *I'll no longer struggle with the mystery.*

My mother agreed to talk, yet when I asked my first question, she snapped, "I don't know what else I can tell you." My hand tightened on the phone, but I suppressed my frustration and ended the call.

In retrospect, I realize that I wanted to reenter that procedure room with my mother and freeze the frame, as you might in editing film. *Are you sure?* I wanted to ask. *You've already tried to end this pregnancy once and it didn't work. Perhaps it's a sign. This baby you have conceived wants to be born.*

I asked my mother how she recovered from her fourth abortion. "My stomach was totally flat again. I felt greatly relieved, greatly relieved, because I was working as a doctor. I certainly wanted to terminate the pregnancy." She didn't allow herself to feel anything else at that point, her ability to suppress her emotions long-established.

She went on to say, "The sadness about the killed . . . the dead fetus . . . was a dead baby practically, it was a late abortion . . . that sadness only started years later."

I notice her struggle for clarity, the words she used: "killed," "dead," "late abortion." Each word an assault.

During our conversation, I repeatedly asked for confirmation that my father had performed the abortion, even though I knew this to be true. I will always yearn for a different answer, one that would have spared my father—spared both my parents—by placing another physician in that procedure room, one whose sole concern was providing excellent patient care.

The timing of the abortion haunts me, as it eventually haunted my mother. Here, too, I wish for a different story, one that would have ended in the procedure room a few weeks into the pregnancy, the abortion complete.

When I asked my mother if her last abortion made her feel differently about abortion in general, she said, "No, it didn't. The only thing is, let's say. To have a baby by a father whom you love, I'm against abortion in that case." So, what am I to make of that? Her response suggests she wishes she had made a different choice.

My mother said her fourth abortion "left a deep scar, a really deep scar on [her] soul." It led her to imagine her child. And in her imagining, she recognized whom she had lost.

"I sometimes wonder, if that baby would have lived, it was a boy, what he would have been like."

After the miscarriage, my father and mother never talked again about the abortion. Perhaps they believed silence was the best way to put it to rest. The reverse was likely true. Whatever my parents felt about the abortion—anger, guilt, remorse—remained unrecognized, and so would seek recognition in their marriage and within the family they created.

"When an inner situation is not made conscious, it happens outside as fate," wrote Carl Jung. What we do not allow to come into being will make its presence felt. Sometimes it seems to me that my shadow brother has always been there, on the periphery of our family as unacknowledged grief.

After my brother Billy was born, my mother wanted to have a tubal ligation to prevent any future pregnancies. Billy's birth had satisfied my father's desire for a son and my mother decided that three children completed their family.

At the time, female sterilization required medical justification and was generally performed only if a future pregnancy would be hazardous to the mother, leaving physicians with some discretion. The chief of the medical staff at Penn, on what my mother believed to be religious and moral grounds, refused to allow Penn physicians to perform the procedure. Furious at this interference with what she viewed as her right, my mother considered having the tubal ligation completed at another hospital. "But then I decided not to do it, although I could have," she told me. "And then I had Henry, which made me very happy."

My mother went on to say, "What really annoyed me later . . . Dad used to tell Henry that I wanted to abort him. Well, I never wanted to abort him. I was only annoyed that my tubes had not been tied."

Henry wasn't my father's target in this exchange, despite the pain it must have caused. My father wanted to hurt my mother, so he weaponized my youngest brother. This particular attack—recasting my mother's desire for a tubal ligation as abortion—likely related to my father's repressed and complicated feelings about having terminated their first pregnancy years earlier. Did he view my mother's choice then as a rejection of him? Or was his resentment the result of his own regret?

My parents entered their marriage having destroyed something between them, though I doubt they considered the abortion in those terms. And yet, I wonder about the long-term effects on their relationship. The abortion may have been a kind of unseen fault line, one that would widen and eventually contribute to the instability of their marriage.

Learning that I might have had an older brother had my parents made a different choice stunned me, and, at the same time, made me feel as though a critical piece in a puzzle had fallen into place. My presence suggested, to both my parents, an absence. In a way, my phantom brother turned me into the shadow, casting me as an inferior version, a poor imitation. This seemed especially true of my father. I had the feeling I disappointed him long before I could have articulated the sentiment. That sensibility encouraged a distance between us impossible to bridge during the years we had together.

After I was born, but before my mother and I came home from the hospital, my father returned alone to our rental house. A clear autumn day, the leaves just beginning to hint at the colors to come, the air warm but with that cool edge that speaks of change. Neighbors' windows are open to a freshening breeze.

As my father approaches the front door, the closest neighbor, whom I will call Sam, leans out his window, eager for news. "Doctor," he says, "has your wife had the baby? What was it?" Without looking at Sam, my father responds, "A girl." He doesn't wait for Sam's reaction before entering the house.

My mother laughed as she repeated the last line, the story being one she offered to illustrate my father's unique sense of humor, but the anecdote leaves me considering how my birth affected him. When he gazed at me, his daughter, whom did he see? Did I remind him of his lost son?

My father died years before I learned of the brother I might have had, so I never spoke to him about any of this. I am not sure I would have dared to do so then even if I'd had the chance. But if he were alive today, I would take that risk. I would tell him that growing up I'd always believed he had the same expectations of me that he would have had for a son.

His determination to ignore gender made me proud of him. But now I wonder if what I took as equal treatment was, in fact, wishful thinking.

As for my shadow brother's effect on my early relationship with my mother, the connection seems less clear, but I believe it exists.

When I was four months old, my mother stopped breastfeeding me because she developed mastitis and then an abscess. The pain was so intense, she told me, that she asked the surgeon to lance the abscess without anesthesia. Proximity to me, her hungry infant, would have worsened her distress, as her body responded to my need. She literally could not bear to hold me close.

I consider my likely response to my mother's turning away. At sixteen weeks, I had started to watch her face closely, learning to read her emotions. I'd begun to communicate my feelings for her—in the way I waved my arms and kicked my legs at her approach, in the way I relaxed when she held me, in my coos and gurgles in response to her voice. I was falling in love.

She was my sustenance and my comfort, my connection and welcome to the world. When she suddenly stopped nursing and holding me, I would have been despairing.

Breastfeeding wasn't common in the 1950s; in fact, my mother had to insist on doing so in defiance of hospital norms. And she told me that four months was long enough to transmit her antibodies against poliovirus, her primary concern. That said, she breastfed my sister and brothers for about a year, or as long as they each desired, so I assume she had intended to do the same for me.

Three months after she stopped nursing me, she conceived my sister, Lydia. I would have sensed her preoccupation with someone else—the fantasy of the child growing in her womb.

My mother's inability to breastfeed me may have been the physical manifestation of a psychological wound she did not recognize. She abruptly stopped nursing me at sixteen weeks. She miscarried my older brother at sixteen weeks. The synchronicity in timing seems significant. Our rupture, an event that would have felt fatal to me, recalled an earlier death.

On my dresser stands one of the rare photographs of my mother, my sister, and me, the image from the summer of 1956 and published in *The Valdosta Times* on the occasion of a visit to my paternal grandmother. I salvaged the photograph from my mother's box of loose photos and framed it, drawn to it initially because of my likeness to my beautiful mother—the same arched brow, the same almond-shaped eyes.

My mother wears a dark scoop-neck dress that accentuates her wide shoulders, her alabaster skin. She has drawn her hair back in a chignon, the style complementing her high cheekbones. She wears lipstick on her wide mouth, mascara to highlight her long lashes. She tilts her head downward and gazes off to the left, her mouth slightly open, as if lost in thought.

My infant sister nestles on my mother's lap, her head against my mother's left breast. Lydia concentrates on her right foot peeking out from the blanket wrapped around her, as if she has just discovered the appendage.

In the photograph I clutch a stuffed dog, a wire fox terrier, a protective arm across his chest, my other hand gripping his tail. The toy resembles the two terriers I will later love. My mother's right hand is cupped loosely around my leg. I gaze off to the left, looking at whatever has drawn my mother's attention. I am struck by my serious expression, one that suggests a wariness, perhaps typical of a child of eighteen months, but I think it is something more. That watchfulness never left me. I remained the reserved child, the observer rather than participant, the child apart.

The Body as Memoir

It is a spring evening during one of my last visits to Texas, not long before my mother moved to Massachusetts. I sit next to her on the sofa in the living room of her small ranch house, a cardboard box full of loose photographs between us. I want to pay attention to the task at hand, but her fragility distracts me. My mother, who always insisted on good posture, has trouble sitting up straight. Her body is closing in on itself, her shoulders and back caving in while her legs crumble. She suffers from post-polio syndrome, the muscle weakness and atrophy symptoms of her childhood disease.

Earlier that day, in the morning, I slipped past her shadowed bedroom, where she slept curled on her side under the sheet and quilt that doubles as a bedspread. She struggles with insomnia and chronic fatigue, additional symptoms of post-polio syndrome. She lay in the middle of the bed, a woman used to sleeping alone. I wondered, once again, at the difference between solitude and loneliness.

In her galley kitchen, I make coffee and heat milk in a saucepan, pour the coffee and milk into a mug. If she were present, she'd hover, not to offer assistance but to safeguard her kitchen's order. I will wash the mug and saucepan and return them to the cabinet before she awakens. As I sip my coffee, I survey the living room where not much has changed since my last visit to Texas, except that the house and room feel diminished, as if they too were drawing inward.

I notice an addition to her collection of Sandicast dog sculptures: A bull terrier has joined the Doberman pinscher and the Great Dane, the replicas realistic with details true to each breed's standards. As he would have been in life, the bull terrier is her favorite. She always liked the dog's eagerness and slightly outlandish appearance, the small triangular eyes in the egg-shaped head. *These are her pets now*, I think.

Before we turn to the photographs, she shows me where she keeps the key to her safe-deposit box, a copy of her will, and other important legal documents. "When I die," she says, "I want the cheapest arrangements possible. No really, I mean it. There are many schemes. I see it on TV." I nod so she knows I've heard her.

She also wants to show me where she keeps my father's ashes. I acknowledge the tin that resembles an old paint can, the can itself wrapped tightly in plastic, the container alone on a shelf in her closet. When she moved from Philadelphia to Texas more than twenty-five years ago, she carried the tin with her in the car.

My father is buried in Texas, I think, even as I'm struck by this arrangement's oddity. It never occurred to any of us to inter the ashes or scatter them in some place significant to him. Perhaps my mother simply wanted to keep him with her in his now manageable form.

We settle in the living room, withdrawing photographs from the open cardboard box. I write in pencil on the backs: names, places, some detail to capture the subject's significance. Most of these photos are from the war years and set in Latvia or Austria.

My mother pauses, fingers the edge of one photograph, holds it out for my inspection. "This is the man, my father's friend, who raped me," she says, her identification dispassionate, as though the rape were merely a way to categorize him.

I would have been stunned at her revelation, had my sister not told me about it a year earlier. During one of Lydia's visits to Texas, my mother had revealed the truth about how she had lost her virginity. What shocked my sister then, and confounds me now, goes beyond the rape. From the time we were both teenagers, my sister and I believed a myth of my mother's making. According to that narrative, our mother had been seduced by an older man, a close friend of her father. Her story contained elements of romance—a sophisticated older man awakens a young woman's sexuality.

I will name this man Emil. He prefers to call my young mother Grietina. The diminutive lacks the protective hardness of Margrieta. Grietina sounds soft when spoken, almost like a caress. He would have wanted her to think of his behavior in that way, as something gentle. Later, if he considers what happened, he will tell himself that she desired him, that he didn't take her by force.

The doorbell surprises Grietina from her reading, as she had not expected any visitors on this damp and chilly late afternoon, suspended between spring and winter. Her parents aren't at home, Lee visiting her mother and Paul occupied with business at the college.

A frown deepens the lines on Emil's face. He worries the brim of the hat he holds in his hand, considers leaving. He had wanted to talk to Paul about Germany's recent invasion of Czechoslovakia, aggression that has gone unanswered, though it's not the end of Germany's ambitions. Latvia remains on the periphery of these events, but that calm will not last. Some believe war is inevitable. What will his old friend say? Emil had looked forward to sharing a drink and intelligent conversation, a chance to recover his calm.

Grietina invites him into the apartment's warmth. She has been schooled not to let a visitor, and certainly not a family friend, depart without some refreshment. Emil is easily persuaded. He's known Grietina since childhood but cannot remember the last time he saw her. *When did the plump girl with Paul's strong features grow into loveliness? Why, she's a young woman now.*

He follows her into the parlor and sits at one end of the curved leather sofa, in front of which stands a round walnut table covered in a lace cloth. He notices the porcelain vase with three long-stemmed roses. *Ah, a woman's touch*, he thinks, and, not for the first time, *Paul is a lucky man.*

Grietina offers him black balsam currant liqueur, the vodka-based aperitif with a bittersweet taste for which Riga is famous. From the glass-fronted cabinet, she retrieves a crystal tumbler and the black bottle with the silver lettering.

"Aren't you going to join me?" he asks. "I don't want to drink alone."

Grietina hesitates, but then takes a small flute from the cabinet. She pours chokeberry wine into her glass, puts both glasses on a silver tray. She sets the tray on the table and sits at the sofa's other end so she can face him. He hands her the crystal flute and raises his own glass to touch hers. "To your health," he says.

Sipping the fortified wine, Grietina feels older than sixteen.

She will not remember the moment when the man she trusted disappeared, replaced by a predator smelling of alcohol and despair. She thinks that if she could identify the moment, she might change the story.

⚜ ⚜ ⚜

In a photograph of Margrieta taken in summer of 1939, the room's window is blacked out by a heavy shade—the war already hovering over this evening. She sits on a banquette next to a handsome man with chiseled features. Her mother sits across from them on the other side of the linen-draped table, its square surface crowded with the remains of coffee and brandy. Margrieta ignores her coffee, doesn't hear her mother's comments. She's too aware of the man sitting next to her, his physical grace, the woody scent of his cologne.

She wears a printed dress and what looks to be a coral necklace at her throat. She has draped her jacket over her shoulders in a way she hopes looks casual but elegant. She doesn't smile, nor does anyone else at the table, as if the photographer has somehow intruded. Her mother, though also lovely, doesn't draw your gaze as Margrieta does, and this may be the first time such a thing is true. Beauty, she is beginning to sense, doesn't belong to her mother alone.

On the back of the photograph, my mother wrote, "Me, 16, madly in love with a Swede, 42, in a nightclub by the sea." As far as I know, the Swede did not return her feelings, but, in parting, he sent my young mother flowers. He may have wanted to compliment the woman she would become. Her mother, accustomed to attention from men, assumed the flowers were for her and wouldn't have appreciated being told otherwise.

I would accept my mother's assertion that she was "madly in love" at sixteen except for something I see in Margrieta's expression. Her eyes reflect what looks to me like disappointment, a melancholy I would not expect in someone so young.

When I look for the source of my young mother's sadness, I return to that gray afternoon a few months earlier. I wonder if this dashing Swede's allure had less to do with his charm and far more to do with the damage inflicted by her father's close friend. Did she believe this older man might erase the pain of that assault? Was her infatuation with the Swede a form of denial?

"Did you tell anyone he'd raped you?" I ask.

"No, not at first, I couldn't think of what to say; he was a trusted family friend," she explains. "And he left me alone after that."

Later, she told her mother, though her father never knew. And Margrieta only revealed the assault because her mother confronted her about her virginity. Lee suspected she was no longer a virgin, possibly because she recognized her infatuation with the Swede and grew suspicious. When Margrieta denied having sex, Lee threatened to take her to a doctor to confirm her claim. To avoid what must have felt like further humiliation, she told her mother about the attack.

"Lee wanted to kill him," my mother said. Apparently, my mother wasn't the first young woman Emil had assaulted. Rumors circulated about his abuse, but no one ever confronted him.

On the back of the photograph I write, "My grandfather's friend." I don't put down "rapist." I will remember.

Rape is a perversion of a physical encounter that holds such potential for good, and its psychological consequences are complicated and long-lasting. I suspect my young mother felt guilt and shame, as do many victims. She might have wondered if she had been at fault because she had somehow encouraged Emil. Maybe she could have stopped him. Maybe he had not attacked her; it only felt that way. She doesn't have a vocabulary for what happened, and no one to help her find the words.

My mother was raped at sixteen and, in all likelihood, again during the war. Of these multiple attacks, I believe the first was the more devastating, because she was not yet an adult. That assault corrupted her first sexual experience, twisting it from intimacy to violation.

For most of her life, my mother denied her rape, in the sense that she could not allow herself to feel the pain of what had happened to her. She constructed a myth of seduction to protect her psyche. But her false narrative had consequences.

When my sister, Lydia, was sixteen and a junior in high school, she fell in love with her English teacher, or at least that's how she characterized her feelings at the time. Fearful he would dismiss her as some silly girl with a crush, she asked our mother if she should tell him how she felt. Our mother encouraged her to do so, and with her knowledge, Lydia embarked on an affair with her much older teacher.

I struggle to explain our mother's rationale—*Lydia will do what she wants and it's better if I know about it . . . He's a teacher and someone I can trust to be protective of my daughter*, or, far more disturbing, *At least Lydia's first lover will be a mature and experienced man, because that's preferable to some fumbling adolescent*. Nowhere in her reasoning did our mother ask herself if what she was encouraging amounted to sexual abuse. And she certainly did not consider how her own rape at sixteen influenced her behavior toward my sister. That said, Lydia's affair may have been as close as our mother could get, on an unconscious level, to her own truth. Repetition was her way of remembering.

Our mother played a role in my sister's victimization. Her advice put Lydia in a situation not unlike the one in which she had found herself at sixteen. Lydia wasn't raped by a trusted older man, as was our mother, but my sister's affair with her teacher overwhelmed her last two years of high school and continued to engulf her long after the relationship had ended. And like my mother's rapist, my sister's teacher had other victims.

I found his obituary recently, and it contains praise for the fine husband and father he'd been, even messages from former students thanking him. I am inclined to dismiss the accolades, but that would be simplistic. He may have been a gifted teacher—those talents fueled my sister's infatuation—but he was also a predator.

When I first learned of my sister's sexual abuse—and I cannot recall how I came to know—I thought of the relationship as an affair. Had she told me about what was going on with her teacher at the time, I would have been impressed, perhaps envious, imagining her as more feminine and worldly than I. But she didn't tell me, at least not during those years.

Lydia and I had stopped confiding in each other before either of us reached puberty. Neither of us would have known how to find emotional support in the other. When the affair ended, as a result of Lydia learning that her teacher was having sex with another student, my sister disappeared into her bedroom. I didn't notice her absence.

Looking back on junior high school and then high school, I realize I could have fallen victim to the predatory behavior of two teachers.

In the first instance, I found myself alone with my seventh-grade teacher in the apartment he shared with his wife. I do not remember how I came to have my new bathing suit with me. Perhaps I'd run into him outside his apartment on my walk home from our neighborhood swim club. I liked this handsome young teacher. He was a Penn graduate, and at that time I hoped to attend Penn, an ambition he encouraged.

He asked me to show him my bathing suit. I did. Then he asked me to try it on for him. Though I felt a warning, I must have gone into the bathroom and changed into the suit, for I see myself standing before him in the black one-piece, aware of an energy in him I could not interpret, but that made me uneasy. In my memory, his wife arrived home and the spell was broken. What would have happened if she had not come home then? The memory ends there with me in the bedroom, staring at my teacher. Did I meet his wife? I think I did. Was I still wearing the bathing suit? I think I wasn't. But her return changed the feeling in the room and ended permanently the connection between my teacher and me.

During my sophomore year in high school, the school's Spanish teacher asked if he could take photographs of me. I am not sure how I came to his attention, as I studied French rather than Spanish, and I do not remember being in his class. But I knew that in addition to teaching Spanish, he was an amateur photographer and had photographed some of my classmates. His request flattered me. I believed he had noticed something special in me, but perhaps he'd merely recognized some vulnerability he could exploit—my desire to be seen.

We arranged to meet at his home outside of school hours, most likely on a Saturday morning. I wore bell-bottom jeans and a long-sleeved, button-down cotton shirt in a muted paisley pattern. He had a makeshift studio set up, a blank white wall behind the stool on which he asked me to sit, a camera on a tripod he stood behind. He asked me to unbutton my shirt's top two buttons. I did. He encouraged me to look at the camera, to move the upper part of my body in response to his repetition of "That's right. Beautiful." I felt as if I had been invited to flirt, but with the camera, not him. And then he said, "Now, I'd like to see you bare to the waist." I'm not sure I said anything in response, but I rebuttoned my shirt and left his apartment. What would have happened if he had been someone other than a short, fat Spanish teacher? What would have happened if he'd looked like my seventh-grade teacher? Would I have done what he wanted? And where would that have led me?

I never told anyone about these two events. Not my father, not my mother. No one.

⚜ ⚜ ⚜

During our discussion about abortion, I asked my mother, "Mom, what would you have done if Lydia or I would have come to you about an abortion?"

"Absolutely for it, if you were very young."

I've no doubt that's true, because she would have responded to an unwanted pregnancy with pragmatism, not judgment.

"Let's say this, when you were sixteen, I told you that I would prefer that you didn't lose your virginity until you were more mature, but things might happen sometimes, and, therefore, I put you both on birth control pills. Remember?"

I tense at her words; my agitation interferes with my ability to listen. This turn in the conversation surprises me. I do not remember any of this—not her advice to wait to have sex, nor her preemptive step in case I didn't.

"I didn't want you to come to me at age sixteen and say, 'Mom, I'm pregnant.'"

At sixteen, I didn't have a boyfriend and did not feel his absence. The public high school for girls I attended afforded me few opportunities to develop relationships of any kind with boys my own age. I would not have asked my mother for contraceptives. So why did she remember that time differently? The answer may lie in her reference to my age: sixteen. My sister's and my adolescent sexuality awakened my mother's memories of her own, one that had been shaped by trauma.

In *The Unsayable: The Hidden Language of Trauma*, clinical psychologist Annie G. Rogers argues that people unconsciously repeat their trauma to fill in an unknown history. What is unsayable insists on some other expression. Lydia and I each took on different aspects of our mother's experience. In Rogers's terms, we each *expressed* what she could not. My sister acted out the myth my mother had created to shield herself, a story of romantic love between an older man and a young woman. As her oldest daughter, I embodied what lay deeper, the wounds she had hidden from herself.

⚜ ⚜ ⚜

I stand at the threshold of the shadowed living room in my friend Jackie's apartment. I wear what used to be called loungewear, an ill-fated cross between cocktail attire and a nightgown. The floor-length silky polyester dress has long sleeves and a scoop neck and smells of Jackie's perfume. I feel newly confident, but also self-conscious, even a little ridiculous. Part of me understands that what is about to occur has been staged by Jackie, including providing the costume I wear.

Jim is several years older. He works in marketing for a local pharmaceutical company. Years later, I will wonder why a man in his mid-twenties would want to date a seventeen-year-old high school senior. At the time, though, I am thrilled to have captured his attention.

When I join Jim on the living room sofa, we will be left alone to begin whatever may develop between us. I don't remember a kiss, perhaps only the anticipation of one. What I remember most clearly was my sudden conviction to go on a diet. I would lose weight to make myself more alluring to Jim, even though he seemed interested in me as I was. I had been ridiculed about being overweight, so I felt vulnerable on this score. When not teased outright, I'd been told that I would be pretty if I lost weight. Beauty might be within reach if I transformed my body.

I lost fifteen pounds in the final months of high school, slender for the first time. Jim didn't comment on my figure then, though toward the end of our relationship, after I'd regained much of the weight I'd lost, he criticized the shape of my thighs. His distaste stung, but I didn't let him see that.

My mother had some role in my meeting Jim, as I recall her telling me that she'd asked Jackie, who was also my father's secretary, to introduce me to a suitable young man. *Suitable for what?* I want to ask now. Was my mother trying to orchestrate how I lost my virginity? Was she trying to protect me from the harm she had experienced, while, at the same time, rewriting her own history by constructing a different one for me? Regardless of what motivated her, I am left with the feeling that she violated boundaries she should have respected. She cast a shadow over a landscape I wanted to discover on my own.

I fell into the idea that my first sexual experience would be with Jim, not because of deepening feelings for him—they remained superficial—but because I'd fixated on the idea of losing my virginity, as if sex were merely a necessary and logical step to enlarge my world.

On a weekend I would have otherwise spent at my high school graduation, I went to the Jersey Shore with Jim. I remember the sound of waves pounding the beach, the sun's heat, the soft grit of sand I let slip through my fingers. I remember the ocean's cold churning water, its salty stickiness as it dried on my skin.

I do not remember Jim clearly, except for his nude body, and only because I'd never seen an adult male naked. Below the waist he looked as if he were wearing furry briefs. I wondered if this was normal.

The clean, but worn, beachfront motel room felt shabby in a way that would have been depressing without the ocean's proximity. It smelled vaguely of mildew from years of wet bathing suits hung to dry or dropped in a damp heap on the carpeted floor. The dim lights and drawn curtains cast the room in a kind of perpetual twilight.

I remained more observer than participant in Jim's and my attempted coupling, my interest in sex clinical. Despite the K-Y Jelly he'd brought along, sexual intercourse proved impossible. And that was the goal, I recognize now, rather than physical intimacy. Jim might have introduced other ways for us to enjoy each other, but he didn't. I wasn't disappointed—I didn't know what I was missing.

About a month after our weekend at the Jersey Shore, I left Jim to go to France for several weeks to see friends I'd made on a study abroad trip the summer before. What I remember most about our parting was how little it affected me. Excited about returning to France, I didn't worry about the effect my absence would have on my relationship with Jim. In truth, I didn't care.

I received a letter from my mother while overseas, about which I remember only this: "Write Jim." Her directive irritated me. *Why would he be talking to my mother?* I wondered. *How is this her business? Does he think she can make me do what he wants?* I didn't call or write.

My relationship with Jim fizzled after my return at summer's end. I learned later from my mother that he believed me to be frigid, an assessment that may have had as much to do with him as with me, though perhaps I am inclined to look at it that way because, in the end, I do not remember him with fondness.

Jim's opinion didn't bother me, as I invested him with little credibility. What upset me was the fact that he'd felt free to discuss his views with my mother and she felt inclined to tell me.

I doubt my mother welcomed this conversation. That it happened might be entirely the result of Jim's own lack of discretion, but I wonder how he came to speak to her and whether something in her behavior led him to believe she was approachable on this subject.

As it turned out, Jim's assessment was wrong, but may have hinted at a different truth. I was not unwilling to engage in sexual activity; I was physically incapable of doing so. And yet, I wonder if my body's response related to an unconscious need for self-protection. Had I absorbed from my mother the sense that physical intimacy posed a threat?

In autumn, as part of a routine gynecological exam, the doctor told me that because of a thick and stiff hymen, sexual intercourse would be, at best, difficult. As a college freshman, I underwent a hymenectomy, a minor surgical procedure to address the problem. I lost my virginity under anesthesia, oblivious. Yet, even if my experience had been a more traditional one—and with someone appropriate in age and sensibility—I recognize now that a part of me would have remained at a remove.

While my mother was working at Methodist Episcopal Hospital in South Philadelphia, she encountered a patient who made her think about the debilitating effects of living with chronic fear. I can picture this elderly Italian lady, alert and inquisitive, drawn to my mother's youth and its attendant loveliness. Something about my mother perplexed her. "You are young and beautiful. Why are you always so scared?" When my mother responded that she was not afraid of anything, the woman said, "But you always have such a scared expression."

A recurrent nightmare, one that would cause my mother to sleepwalk, plagued her around this same time. In the dream, she finds herself in Riga's Ministry of Transportation, the building that housed her godfather's apartment. He worked as a senior official within the Ministry, responsible for the Latvian rail system. She is walking down a corridor at night, the lights dim. Closed doors line the walls and high ceilings arch overhead. Her footsteps echo on the marble floors. As she proceeds, the corridor grows gradually narrower. She knows that one of the doors will eventually open, and she will see Soviet soldiers, "the ultimate horror."

When my mother told me about this dream, she also said that she now believed that she had been suffering from post-traumatic stress disorder (PTSD) when she arrived in the United States, the recurring nightmare being the symptom that led to her self-diagnosis.

The nightmares eventually ended, and with their cessation, my mother believed she had recovered.

The psychiatric field did not formally recognize PTSD until 1980, some thirty years after my mother's immigration, and therapies developed at that time were narrowly focused on combat veterans. Since then, the disorder and its complex variations have become a well-established part of the diagnostic canon. Psychiatry's understanding of the nature of trauma and its effects on the body, brain, and mind has deepened and expanded, as have therapeutic responses.

I believe my mother's diagnosis was correct, but we disagree about her recovery. My mother endured multiple injuries before my birth—parental abuse, the devastation and humiliation of war, rape—wounds she buried in order to survive. But trauma unacknowledged doesn't disappear. It resurfaces like a dormant virus.

In *The Body Keeps the Score*, Bessel van der Kolk explains that traumatized people feel chronically unsafe in their bodies. In this sense, the body remembers what cannot be expressed in words. My mother did not feel safe in her body, and as a result, could not communicate that ease to me as her child. Her traumatic history corrupted our earliest interactions, weakening our nascent bond.

As her firstborn living child and female, I acted as a kind of mirror for my mother, reflecting back to her a painful past she could not acknowledge. She turned away from that history, and that meant she withheld herself from me in some fundamental ways. She did so unconsciously and so could not undo it. And because this happened before I had language to comprehend it, my only possible response was instinctual. I withdrew.

Bessel van der Kolk, in reference to the work of John Bowlby and other researchers in attachment, affirms that a child's earliest caregiver shapes how the child's rapidly growing brain perceives reality. In response to her caregiver, the child develops an inner map that forms the template of how she thinks of herself and the world around her. Given that the self is the primary reference point for a very young child, when her caregiver cannot adequately meet her needs, that child internalizes the idea that something is wrong with her.

I do not know when I first developed an idea of the contours of my inner world, but I do remember that I found comfort in my belief that a part of me remained unreachable. Throughout my adolescence, what I would now describe as a kind of assertive invulnerability felt like a strength. If I did not need anyone, I would not be disappointed. If I could not be touched, I would remain safe. If no one knew my deepest feelings and thoughts, they would remain mine.

When I was already an adult, my mother told me two things about my early childhood that have stayed with me. The first was that I had been "unusually attached" to her as a child. At first, I thought she meant that I had been possessive, or had loved her with a particular ferocity. But I now think that what she interpreted as an uncommon attachment was, in fact, a yearning for her that was never satisfied.

She also described how brave I had been as a young child during times of stress. "You could be sick all night and you would never call for me," she remembered. I suspect that my apparent stoicism was not bravery but resignation. I was learning to be alone.

Pine Street

My brothers, my sister, and I all grew up in an old rambling house on a tree-lined street within walking distance of the University of Pennsylvania Hospital, where my father pursued his medical career. According to my mother, my father, "the boss," made the decision to buy the house, yet I do not associate him with the place. His comings and goings were like a wind. Gusts could be disruptive, sometimes energizing, but they did not last. My mother endured, so I connect Pine Street with her.

She found the house beautiful with its high ceilings, generous windows, and hardwood floors. She noted the architectural details—crown molding in the living room, beveled glass around the front and side doors. The house impressed her as full of possibility.

For a time, she worked to enhance our surroundings by removing wallpaper, plastering and painting rooms, refinishing furniture she had acquired at resale shops or at auction. I was too young then to appreciate her aspirations. I remember Pine Street in disorder and disrepair, though occasionally I could see the elegant bone structure beneath the neglected surface.

As did everyone in the family, I referred to our house as "Pine Street," offering a partial address by way of identification. That seems so apt now, the name revealing more than I recognized. One of the meanings of *pine* is "to yearn." Our years there were characterized by longing, a hunger for things I could not name.

Built in 1925, the house has been sold twice in the last forty-five years, the first time in January 1981, when my mother moved to Texas, the second time a few years later. I looked it up on a realtor's website and found it listed as a multifamily dwelling with an apartment available for rent. I recognized my paternal grandmother's old apartment in the description of the second-floor unit with a separate entrance, perfect for a student.

It struck me as fitting, this carving up of our former home into rental housing for transitory residents, each living apart from the others, as if the house's layout had finally caught up with the way we had inhabited that space. I lived at Pine Street for more than twenty years, longer than anywhere else, but our family home felt temporary. Instead of settling there, we camped.

Pine Street's shuttered white face rose above a steep flight of stone steps I had trouble climbing as a child. A rickety metal handrail bordered the steps on the left, and on the right the sloping ground was dense with ivy.

Once, when I was six or seven, I pushed my sister, Lydia, down those steps. I cannot recall doing it and so cannot explain my motivation, as Lydia then was usually more playmate than target. When confronted by my father, who must have witnessed the shove, I said, "I didn't mean to hurt her." When he responded that I did *indeed* mean to hurt her, I defended myself, "Yes, but not that bad." He nodded, apparently satisfied. He may have valued the fact that I told the truth more than he disapproved of my aggression. My sister recovered without difficulty and probably found some way to get even. As children, we had our own rules of engagement, and our parents did not intervene.

I like to think they would have intervened if they had known about the hanging. Henry was about four, so I would have been about nine. Our parents were out, and they had enlisted a nurse who worked at the hospital to babysit. Early in the evening, we recognized that we could ignore her; in fact, she seemed to want to be left alone.

Lydia, Billy, and I decided to play a game. Henry, the youngest and still too small to assert himself, had to take whatever role we assigned him. In this case, he was the condemned. We sat him down, probably in the bedroom Lydia and I shared, because it was as far away from the babysitter as possible. Not being able to envision any kind of legal proceeding, or the crimes for which we intended to hold Henry accountable, we emphasized that his offenses were many and that the trial had been a long and careful process. We had arrived at a verdict, and though we regretted it, we had no alternative: Henry would be hanged. We had no idea about the next steps, but following through was not our intent. The ruse ended there, with the threat.

Well into adulthood I thought the story amusing, an example of our imaginative play. I also believed that the allure violence and fear held for us made us typical children. What I didn't understand until recently is that Henry had believed we were going to hang him. That evening, he learned watchfulness. To trust us meant risking destruction.

My father devised a different game, a more elaborate one, but also one dependent on fear. As a member of the Army Reserve, he periodically participated in training for how to handle major trauma—gaping wounds, chemical burns, limbs nearly severed. To provide as realistic an experience as possible, those assigned roles as victims wore latex body parts through which embedded tubes could pump red dye. Faces, hands, torsos—flayed and mutilated.

My father donned his costume, drew the living room's drapes, and then turned off the main breaker controlling our electrical power. We played in the dark. He prowled the house, sometimes waiting around a corner or in a closet, though he lacked the patience to stay silent and still for long. My siblings and I formed a unit to begin our search, no one brave enough to venture off alone.

I murmured "Daddy" as I stepped forward, alert to the creak of the floor, the sound of a door opening in the corridor. I both wanted and did not want to find him. We whispered to each other, asking ourselves if that was his step we heard, that moan real or imagined. Billy and Henry retreated first, the tension too much, so that by the end, Lydia and I were the only searchers left. Sometimes we found him or he us, but more often we could not sustain our nerve.

My mother's passive presence in the game created the safe space to which we could retreat. She reclined on the daybed in the living room waiting for us, knowing our fear would escalate and we would go to her. In the darkness, the glow of her cigarette a lighthouse calling ships home.

My father translated battlefield training into a game with his children, something that strikes me now as problematic.

Even without our game, that suitcase of mutilated body parts fascinated me. I wanted to understand what had yielded such trauma. The same desire led me to look through my father's medical books, alighting on photographs of ghastly injuries.

It's telling that Charles Addams was one of my parents' favorite cartoonists—they passed on that preference. His intelligent and artistic drawings appeared regularly in the pages of *The New Yorker*, starting in the 1930s through early 1993. Many of his cartoons don't have captions, leaving the interpretation up to the viewer. One I remember well features several members of the Addams Family gathered on the roof of their grim Victorian, from which they tilt a cauldron of boiling oil toward unsuspecting carolers below. The drawing is only funny because the oil never reaches those singers. Its humor comes from considering how far the Addams Family's idea of holiday cheer diverges from the norm.

Another cartoon that never fails to amuse me shows Morticia Addams opening the front door to find a befuddled mailman delivering two wire cages, a child in each. She calls out to an eager Gomez, telling him their children have returned from camp. Like Morticia and Gomez, my parents loved their children but had a dubious grasp of parenting.

The other reason I remember this drawing is because the children are in cages. I slept in a drawer as an infant. When I learned of this as an adolescent, I remember wondering how it all worked. *Was the drawer part of a dresser and did my mother close, or partially close, the drawer from time to time? Was I literally put away?* Later, I realized that the drawer must have been placed on a table or the floor, but still. My parents had nine months to prepare, couldn't they have managed a crib?

I suspect that the nature of our games and those cartoons fit a larger familial pattern. A preoccupation with the macabre. Some unmet need led us to focus on death and injury. Our play, as well as our shared humor, may have represented unrecognized trauma transformed into something that could be addressed indirectly, and in that way, preserved within our family. We needed to return to what had not been resolved.

At the top of Pine Street's stone steps, a brick walkway framed the side and front of the house, separating the wooden porch from a small yard dominated by three hydrangea bushes and two pine trees.

A large door opened from the porch into a foyer, at the end of which a second door exited into the hallway adjacent to the living room. This must have been the house's primary entrance at some point, but none of us used it that way. Instead, my mother installed hanging rods between the two doors and transformed the foyer into her closet.

I sometimes ventured into the forbidden space to let stiff, satiny fabric brush by my face in the dark. The spice of my mother's perfume drew me forward, until the sharp bite of mothballs drove me away.

Her renovation forced everyone to use the side door to enter the house. When visitors and deliverymen persisted in trying the still-prominent front door, she put a porch swing in front of it, a practical, if not visually appealing, solution. Not until decades later did I realize how disorienting this arrangement had been, even unwelcoming. And I see too how the absence of a clear entrance to our house mirrored my mother's and my relationship.

Pine Street told a story about my family—not only in the ways in which we used the house's interiors but also in the ways we shaped and cared for domestic space. Though my years there included other narratives, it is our failure to create a place of comfort and nurture that I remember, a place I would call home.

If you wandered into the living room, you might find a metal lawn chair, the vinyl cover fraying, next to a worn leather couch. Two Eames chairs sat near a large teak coffee table of Scandinavian design, the chairs and table the only pieces that seemed to have been chosen for aesthetic appeal. The wooden floors, unprotected, showed rough patches where splinters trapped bare feet. An enormous mirror shone from the hallway, so that as you moved through the space you would catch glimpses of yourself.

In one corner of the living room, my father's leather recliner stood next to a lamp. During the years he still lived at Pine

Street, he sat there sometimes, *The New England Journal of Medicine* in his hands. While he read, he liked for me to massage his head. I grew bored quickly, so as an inducement for me to continue, he would pay me.

I straddled the back of the chair, sitting comfortably above my father's head and shoulders, my feet just touching the tops of his arms. I moved my hands in circles across his scalp, scratching his head of thinning hair. My fingers grew slick, flakes of dandruff drifting down over his shoulders. He paid me a penny a minute, a bargain that seemed promising. I knew better than to disturb his reading, because he would tell me to be quiet. Instead of talking to my father, I daydreamed, *How long will it take me to earn a dollar? What will I do with such a sum?*

Pine Street had a formal dining room, but except for Thanksgiving and Christmas, we did not gather there as a family. My father's hours were unpredictable, so meals could not be planned to accommodate him. My mother prepared dinners for my brothers, my sister, and me, but she ate when she felt like it. We often took our plates up to my parents' bedroom, eating in front of the television, sometimes sitting on my parents' bed, other times on chairs dragged in from another room.

Occasionally my mother put food out on the living room's coffee table, but it was too low for comfort. One of my last clear images of a meal in that room comes from my freshman year at Penn. My then boyfriend, another Penn student, had moved from Florida, and I remember thinking I should find a way to offer him a home-cooked meal, so I invited his roommate and him to lunch at Pine Street. My mother prepared steak, baked potatoes, and a green salad. Instead of setting the dining room table, we used the small stacking tables in the living room. When my boyfriend started to cut his steak, he applied pressure to the plate and it shifted, almost crashing to the floor. I remember my relief that it hadn't fallen off the little table, because of how embarrassed he would have been. And yet, I felt embarrassed, by the way we perched in the living room on whatever seats were available, by what I sensed of my mother's discomfort.

Now, when Tom and I entertain, whether it be for cocktails or dinner, I try to plan for everything—the combination of foods, the pacing of the meal, the table setting, seating, lighting—whatever choices might affect our guests' enjoyment, and also, I realize, reflect on my skills as a hostess. It means my efforts lack spontaneity, and until I lose my self-consciousness, I do not relax fully, even with good friends. The gathering retains aspects of a performance, one I will revisit for areas of improvement.

Tom, who put himself through college cooking, always approaches the chance to welcome friends into our home with enthusiasm and confidence. He never seems tense, except in response to my anxiety.

For a few years, my mother claimed the dining room for her sewing projects, demonstrating a degree of care in that work that was otherwise absent.

She purchased expensive fabrics—silks and woolens—knowing she could not afford to make a mistake, and she relied on *Vogue* patterns, readily available in the 1960s. The lined translucent pages fit within a slim paper package, on the package's front a blue banner with "Vogue Couturier Design" in white letters. Below the banner, a photograph of a model wearing the finished clothing, and next to the photo, a stylized drawing of a model wearing the same item but in a different color, sometimes with slight variations in design, a longer sleeve or a raised collar. The drawn model always impossibly thin.

My mother subscribed to a magazine called *Elégance* that contained swatches of fabric for the dresses, gowns, and coats displayed. "See," she would say, touching the samples, "you wouldn't think this dress would work in both jersey and wool tweed, but it does."

She appreciated good craftsmanship in architecture and in fashion. She passed this on to me, especially when it came to clothes. In my early twenties, I used to harass her into shopping with me at the discount places I favored, because I could count on her to distinguish well-made from mediocre. She zeroed in on buttonholes. "Look," she would say, holding a jacket up for my inspection, her forefinger peeking through the already fraying buttonhole, "machine-made and not finished off." Later, when we lived in different parts of the country, I would call her with descriptions of what I had worn to an event with Tom or my recent purchase from a chic boutique, gratified by her interest.

Sometimes I lingered at the dining room's threshold to watch my mother making clothes, impressed by her mastery of what looked to me an incomprehensible puzzle. She would lay the fabric out on the dining room table and place the pattern on top, pinning the two together with the straight pins she held in her mouth. Then, using a tracing wheel, she would outline where she needed to cut the fabric. Once she had the pieces of the dress or jacket ready to assemble, she used her Singer sewing machine to complete the garment.

Even my Barbie benefited from my mother's sewing skills. Clothes for the doll were ridiculously expensive and poorly constructed. In keeping with what she would later advise me to do in regard to my own wardrobe, privileging quality over quantity, she sewed a few outfits scaled to fit the doll. Later, when I was a teenager, she also made some clothes for me—a gray wool skirt that swished when I walked and a long skirt in black-and-white jersey that boosted my confidence.

After my mother had moved to Texas, I would set aside clothing in need of repair or modification in anticipation of her visits. She would reinforce buttons on a coat, mend a seam. In the 1980s, most of my blouses and jackets had shoulder pads, fashionable at the time. I did not like the way the pads shifted around when I wore the garments, so I asked my mother to solve the problem. To hold the pads in place, she put snaps on them, a tedious job. "Thanks, Mom," I'd say, appreciative in an absent-minded way.

The last item of clothing she made for me is something I safeguard, having moved it multiple times from one house to the next. The multicolored polyester robe rests folded at the bottom of a dresser drawer. I have not worn it for decades, but that doesn't matter. It recalls my mother to me, and the ways in which she gave me what she could.

There is an element of optimism in making clothes, especially the elegant ones my mother crafted. The garments represented an investment in the future. At some point, however, while I was in high school, my mother stopped sewing for herself. I thought she had simply lost interest, but I see her behavior differently now. Her abandonment of sewing resulted from an erosion of hope.

Later, after the dining room table no longer served as her work area, I noticed the marks left by the tracing wheel's serrated blade, a sacrifice to my mother's creativity. She paid such close attention to her sewing, methodical during every step, but failed to protect the table's wooden surface. I recognized that the defects need not be permanent—the table could be refinished—but I knew she would not take that step. The damage bothered me, in part, because the table had been a good piece of furniture, but what gnawed at me more was the recognition that I seemed to be the only one who saw the scarring.

When I recall Pine Street, I return to my parents' bedroom, because my mother spent most of her time there. The room's walls were unadorned, the tables devoid of anything decorative or personal. A still-life painting someone had given my parents, lovely and within reach, remained in the closet for years until my mother passed it on to me. The painting, of a fence post on which sits an onion plant, reminds me of Andrew Wyeth's work, with its muted palette and attentiveness to light, space, and texture. I find in the image a melancholy beauty. Perhaps the still life didn't appeal to my mother. Or maybe it stayed in the closet as a result of her own inertia. It hangs now in Tom's and my bedroom.

My parents' high, carved wooden bed occupied the center of the room. An inoperable fireplace marked one wall, windows and closets two others, and a huge mirror the fourth. It would have only required removing the mirror to adjust the bed's location, but that minor renovation was never undertaken. Except for some random pieces of furniture, my parents' bedroom had the vacant, yet expectant, atmosphere of unfinished space. Even before my father departed Pine Street, the room never felt like a place of intimacy.

For a brief period, while I was still an adolescent and just starting high school, we had a lovely cleaning lady who used to come once a week. While she worked for my mother, Pine Street never fell into such disorder that recovery felt impossible. Eventually, though, my father stopped paying this bill, and my mother, without any income of her own, could not afford it. Sometimes one of us would straighten up a single room, usually our own or the living room in anticipation of guests, but no one looked after the entire house.

The kitchen's mess would eventually require a response, and that response most often came from my mother. Dirty dishes accumulated in the sink and then crowded the kitchen counters, leaving space only for the roaches. To prepare food required cleaning dishes, and having begun, it made sense to clean them all. But the kitchen's restoration never lasted, so the cycle would begin again.

I search for an explanation, or an excuse, for why I never helped my mother. She didn't ask for assistance, but that should not have been necessary. I didn't feel responsible for what I experienced as Pine Street's chaos; I just wanted to flee.

Pine Street seemed to shrink, its inhabited spaces growing smaller and more isolated. We each retreated to wherever felt like refuge—my father to his work at the hospital and his relationships there, and I to the one space I thought belonged to me, my bedroom. Too caught up in my own frustration and unhappiness, I didn't notice how my brothers and sister responded.

Painted the vivid color of a yellow cab, my bedroom gleamed, as though lit from within. The large room had three windows and a Dutch door that led out onto a relatively flat roof. In summer, I sunbathed there on an old chaise lounge, the aluminum armrests hot in the sun, my body slippery with suntan oil. The pungent, peppery scent of my sweat, the edible fragrance of coconut, and the smell of tar enveloped me as I dozed in the heat.

From my room I gazed out the open Dutch door to the trees and roofs of neighboring houses. I transformed myself into a bird, flying from tree to tree, never touching the ground. Flight required only the courage to relax my body and fall forward, arms extended. One act of faith, and I would be airborne, elsewhere.

A wasting apathy settled on Pine Street. I couldn't have described it that way at the time, but I remember some of its effects.

One afternoon, I came upon our old cat circling her empty bowl in the grimy kitchen. Her hip bones carved her flanks in a way that looked painful. I knew from her plaintive meowing that she was desperately hungry, but I just stood there. I never bothered to feed her, my neglect increasing her suffering. Her vulnerability and need irritated me. It was as if I had to make another creature, one weaker than I, a target for what I now see as anger.

We never bothered to spay our cat, allowing her to produce litters of kittens from time to time. I don't remember what happened to most of them, except the last, but only because a high school friend told me. A neighbor noticed the dead kittens sealed in a plastic bag, discarded in the trash. She pointed them out to my friend as she arrived for a visit, and my friend told me. I do not recall what we said to each other, except my lie. I knew I couldn't deny what she'd seen, so I had to deny that my family had anything to do with it. "How awful," I said. "I have no idea how those poor kittens ended up in our trash. Who would do such a thing?"

My mother had smothered the newborn kittens. She had sealed them in a plastic bag, depriving them of air. I never asked her about it. Had I done so, I expect she would have responded that she'd done the best thing for our aging cat, the kittens too. But I wonder at how she managed to remove herself from feeling during the act. What parts of her had to disappear?

I couldn't have done it, not then and not now, yet I recognize that there's a kind of privilege in my assurance. I never experienced the abuse that could result in my mother's dissociation. Though I tried to retreat to somewhere entirely devoid of feeling, a tiny voice, sometimes not more than a whisper, warned me I didn't belong there.

Leaving Pine Street

My mother wanted an open coffin for her father's funeral, because she thought he looked handsome and distinguished. He hadn't impressed her that way for a long time.

My grandfather died in late summer of 1970 in his bedroom, the one between my sister's and mine on the third floor, where he had lived for some fourteen years. Away working as a mother's helper on Cape Cod, I chose not to return for his funeral. In truth, his death didn't affect me. I had distanced myself years before when I realized I held little interest for him.

Paul was around sixty when he arrived in the United States and never found another job. Whatever professional ambitions he had once possessed became another casualty of the war. My father viewed my grandfather's perpetual unemployment as sloth and used his contempt as a weapon against my mother. Years later, my mother told me she had felt ashamed of her father's financial dependence.

I noticed her disappointment in her silence, in the way she turned away from him as she prepared his dinner, often the same meal of sausages and sauerkraut. While she fried the sausages, my grandfather waited at the far end of the kitchen's wooden picnic table, its surface covered in a sometimes-sticky blue-and-white-checkered oilcloth. As soon as she set his plate down, she departed, leaving him to his solitary meal.

And yet, she loved him. When he lay close to death, most likely from heart failure, she sat beside him holding his hand, telling him he'd recover. He responded that he knew he was dying. She must have known it too but did not want to accept their ending.

I didn't try to comfort my mother. I would not have known how. Whatever grief she felt, she kept to herself, though her father's death must have affected her. He had been the parent whose affection she had never doubted. His death took away his untold stories about the past, and left questions my mother wished she had asked unanswered.

My father's mother, whom we called Granny, also lived with us. She had her own apartment, created on the second floor of a two-story addition my parents constructed at the back of the house. She visited during summers, exchanging Valdosta's humidity for Philadelphia's, and eventually moved in year-round.

My grandmother didn't approve of my mother and used to criticize her for what she viewed as laziness, or, at least, an inattentiveness to the tasks necessary for a smooth-running household. They seemed to have no common ground, not even my father. And because I knew she didn't like my mother, I had to choose sides, even if unconsciously. I chose my mother.

Granny liked me, though, and tried to improve me with piano lessons and Easter dresses. I took to the latter but not the former, though now I wish I had. Whatever malice she possessed, she directed toward Billy, repeating a pattern established between her mother and my father, and like that animosity, without any apparent justification. Granny called Billy "impudent," until, finally, he was. In the same way I avoided our grandfather, Billy learned to stay clear of our grandmother.

Nine months after my grandfather's death, Granny got up in the middle of the night, walked to the threshold of my parents' bedroom, and told my mother, "Margaret, I am having a heart attack." My father wasn't at home, probably on call at the hospital. My mother awakened me to help guide Granny back to her bed. She left me to hold my grandmother, while she went in search of morphine. Groggy from sleep but also confident my mother knew what she was doing, I followed her instructions. Calling an ambulance would have been futile, as the medical field's limited response to heart attacks at the time involved bed rest and pain management—morphine being the preferred option.

I sat on the bed, supporting the upper half of my grandmother's body, her breathing like someone trying to inhale underwater as her lungs filled with fluid. When my mother returned with the syringe ready, she told me I could leave. I waited downstairs, dozing on the couch in the laundry room at the back of the house. "How's Granny?" I asked when my mother reappeared. "She's dead," my mother said. Her flat response didn't surprise me. The news did, because I'd not understood that my grandmother had been dying in my arms. Eight years later, over the phone, my mother will tell me of my father's death in the same blunt way: "Dad is dead," no preamble, just three words with the sharp reverberation of gunshots.

Paul and Granny both died of heart failure, and sometimes I wonder if there exists some deeper meaning in their common affliction. These two people, isolated in different ways, died from hearts broken long before, from whose fracturing they never recovered.

I did not think about how their deaths might affect the life of Pine Street, but now I wonder. It may be that their presence contributed to some kind of familial equilibrium. Once they were gone, what I think of as my family's unmaking accelerated.

My youngest brother also took his leave around this time. A neighbor and the owner of a local bike shop began sexually abusing Henry. My brother would not have characterized Jerry's behavior as child abuse; he once called their relationship love.

I didn't learn of the abuse until years later, but I sensed something off earlier.

My mother had hired Jerry to do some carpentry work in the third-floor bathroom. I remember his even white teeth and self-satisfied grin, his honeyed voice that hinted of a secret just for you. He strode through our house as if he belonged there. Whatever my mother's impairment—and I believe it was considerable—how could she not recognize Jerry as a predator? She'd had experience with other predators.

Returning to my bedroom one day, I found deep cuts in the side of my mahogany desk, the damaged places raw against the dark wood. Jerry had used my desk as his workbench, slicing into the wood as he sawed plywood planks into shorter pieces. Invading my bedroom was, I see now, a different kind of violation.

I was furious, though no one seemed to care. Henry's defense of Jerry made me even angrier. My brother stood before me, his fists clenched, his face pale with barely suppressed rage. I feared he would attack me if I continued my tirade. *What happened to my brother? Who is this unrecognizable boy threatening me?* I thought. I believed that something was wrong with Henry, not that he had been wronged.

Jerry had access to our home for a time. He had access to my mother, whom he treated with casual intimacy. A child abuser found safe harbor in our house, and my mother provided it, unwittingly or not.

I never spoke to my mother about what happened to Henry, abuse that started when he was nine years old and continued until he was thirteen. That said, I believe that she both knew and did not know what was going on. Her drinking progressed during this time, and that would have diminished her mental capacity. But she also resisted recognizing Henry's abuse because to face my brother's victimization put her at risk of acknowledging her own. A kind of toxic self-protectiveness prevented her from protecting my brother.

Jerry molested multiple boys over a period of years, yet no one intervened. As far as I know, none of the boys revealed what was happening to them at the time, their silence typical of the victims of sexual abuse. Yet I am left with the suspicion that Jerry's predatory behavior was a kind of open secret within our community, the protection of which made us all, to varying degrees, complicit.

I have a photograph Jerry took of my brother and me the summer after my freshman year of college, when I was eighteen and Henry twelve. Other people are in the frame, but it's my brother who draws my attention. He is seated, his elbows on his knees, his mouth slightly open. He doesn't look toward the camera; he doesn't seem to be looking at anything. Even if I did not know his history, I would see the emptiness in his dark eyes, an expression that calls to mind grief. Without anyone marking its passage, my brother's childhood had already ended.

Though my leave-taking differed in character, I also departed Pine Street. In the summer of Granny's death, I went to France's Loire Valley on a study abroad program for American high school students, having launched my campaign to do so that spring. At first, my father said he would not pay for the trip, but my mother assured me she would get him to change his mind. She still wielded influence with him, and I trusted her to negotiate on my behalf.

I had started learning French at age twelve, when my otherwise dismal middle school offered students a choice between Spanish and French. I chose the latter, drawn to what I heard as its music. No one in my family had any connection to France or the French language, and that increased the appeal. I could call them my own. I was good at French, naturally so, and study made me better.

When I returned from France at summer's end, my mother picked me up at the Philadelphia airport, the last time she would do so; thereafter, my comings and goings went unnoticed. Before even settling into the car, I announced, "I'm going back." And she responded, "Mission accomplished," a comment that did not resonate with me at the time but does now.

My mother identified herself as European, an assertion that went beyond geography to claim ties to a different culture, and, for her, a formative one. It occurs to me that she wanted to give me the same opportunity—another way of being in the world beyond the confines of our family home.

When I speak of my mother, the first thing I say is, "My mother was Latvian," a statement that has more to do with me than my mother. It is a way of saying I am not of this place, regardless of where I find myself. It gives me a feeling of freedom and possibility. It is, at times, a kind of escape.

In *The Body Keeps the Score*, Bessel van der Kolk writes that the inner map a mother gives her child can be modified by experience, particularly during adolescence. Being in France at age sixteen gave me a more hopeful sense of myself. By helping me leave Pine Street, if only for a summer, my mother may have saved me.

My connection to France began with Didier, a French university student assigned to our high school group that summer. Four years older, he looked like a healthier, taller, and younger version of Mick Jagger. And he could sing. I thought him handsome and talented, a male version of the person I wanted to be. In his eyes, I was the American girl with the long chestnut hair, the lyric soprano voice. It was as if by association some of his shininess rubbed off on me.

I spent my college summers at La Volinière, the farm Didier's parents owned in the Loire Valley, the fertile heart of France. Marie-Thèrese and Damien embraced me, almost from the beginning, surprised that a surgeon's daughter found joy in the rhythm of farm life. I helped where I could, but always gravitated toward the barn. In advance of milking, I'd tie each cow's slapping tail to a hind leg, carrying the soiled twine around my neck so it would be easier to reach. Those messy strings, as much as anything, secured my spot in the family.

During those summer afternoons, Marie-Thèrese introduced me to cheese-making in the farm's cave, a room built of stone with small windows that provided ventilation rather than light. We entered this space through a narrow door off of the kitchen, stepping down two steps into cool stillness. As Didier's mother turned perforated plastic containers of fermenting milk, I followed with a utensil similar to a potato masher to press the thickening mixture deeper into each mold, releasing the accumulated liquid. The sound of water dripping and the scent of fresh cheese accompanied our French lessons. She taught me how to pronounce the French *r*. "*Route*," I'd repeat, my mouth pursed as if in a kiss, and "*rue*," the sound coming from deeper in my throat.

I prized those interludes with Marie-Thèrese and the companionship she offered. She was not so much teaching me to make cheeses or even to speak French. She was sharing aspects of her life and, in doing so, welcoming me. Through Didier's mother I discovered the relaxed closeness possible between an older and younger woman.

I brought Tom to La Volinière after our 1982 wedding. He had never been to France, and it had been seven years since my last visit, though I had seen Didier when he traveled to the United States. I had hoped to return to France sooner, but after finishing college, I got a job—eventually, a series of jobs—and then I went on to graduate school at Wharton.

I felt nervous about Tom's and my visit to the farm. Not because of anxiety about whether Damien and Marie-Thèrese would like Tom. Didier already did, so I knew they would as well. I feared they would find me changed and I them, so that what had been a kind of touchstone for me would no longer be so.

If Tom is describing our visit, he will always say, "You have to understand, this family treated her like a daughter. They wanted her to marry their son." At which point, I remind him I am not sure about that, and, in any case, Didier was gay. "But even so," Tom will add.

As are most celebrations in France, ours was organized around shared food and wine, but before beginning the festivities, Damien wanted to complete some minor chores. Tom offered to help him stock shelves with fruits and vegetables put up over the winter. Since Damien spoke no English and Tom minimal French, I asked him how he had managed.

"It wasn't rocket science," he explained, "I just watched what Didier's father did. The jars were glass. I could see what was inside. Green beans went with green beans, apricots with apricots." When Damien and Tom returned to the living room, he chided me that Tom did indeed understand French, and if I would only spend time helping him, he would learn to speak the language.

We lingered for hours at the laden table. Our feast began with Marie-Thèrese's country pâté, the best I have eaten—savory and rich without the oily taste of liver. During a walk earlier in the day, Tom had asked if fish swam in the stream flowing through the property. As evidence, grilled trout followed the pâté. We continued with roast chicken, fresh peas, and tender roasted potatoes bathed in the chicken's juices, rounded out by green salad and cheese, with a flaky fruit tart for dessert. Virtually everything we enjoyed had been produced on the farm.

Damien kept returning to his wine cellar throughout the meal, eager to introduce Tom to the best pairings of food and wine. I can still recall his delight, his exhortations of "*Goûtez-moi ça*" as he urged Tom to taste the full-bodied red Burgundy with walnuts.

Just before departing, I stood in the kitchen with Marie-Thèrese. She looked up from her work and said with a smile, "*Tu est bien tombée, ma fille*," reminding me I was lucky to have found Tom. From then on, she called him Tom Pouce, after a character from a fairy tale.

A year after my return from my first trip to France, I sit with my parents in one of Philadelphia's Italian restaurants, reluctantly tasting the spongy calf's brain my father insists is delicious. My reluctance extends beyond the meal. We are celebrating my admission to the University of Pennsylvania, though my father is the only one at the table who appears pleased. I do not remember my mother's role in this particular battle, perhaps because she did not have one. The struggle unfolded between my father and me, though the odds were against me from the beginning.

I had wanted to study in France at one of the country's public universities. I didn't have much of a plan beyond that, nor time to prepare one before my father intervened. He said he wouldn't support me. I didn't possess the resources, material or emotional, to defy him.

If I could advise my then-seventeen-year-old self, I would urge her to leave Philadelphia to study elsewhere, even if not in France. I would tell her that her best chance of thriving in college would be at a small liberal arts school, where she could have closer relationships with faculty members. But that would be only part of my reasoning. I needed to leave the city to remove myself from Pine Street. Staying kept me tethered to my mother, even against my will—in resentment and anger, in worry, in the fear that I could not be free until I secured something I could not then describe.

I could tell myself that I remained because I recognized my mother's fragility and need, when it was the reverse. I wanted something from her, from both my parents, that I had yet to receive but still believed they could provide. Assurance of my own competence and confirmation of my worth.

My father's position as a full professor of medicine meant I had free tuition at the university. As a result, he pushed me toward Penn. Much later, I learned that he had feared something might happen to him, and that, in his absence, I would lose my tuition benefits. My father did die before we had all finished college, but Penn honored the commitment, waiving tuition through graduate school.

As an inducement to attend Penn, my father paid for on-campus housing. I did not have to live at Pine Street, but I kept wandering back, my mother's presence there a siren's call.

That dinner in the Italian restaurant turned out to be the last meal I shared with both of my parents together.

I do not know when my father began his affair with Carol, a fellow plastic surgeon nine years his junior. I must have met her early in her tenure at Penn because I retain an image of her pregnant, and her last child was born in 1966, two years after she had come to the university as a resident in plastic surgery.

Her enormous belly—the first thing I noticed—threatened to overwhelm her five-foot frame. Despite that encumbrance, she carried herself with an assertiveness I associated with my father and possessed a way of speaking that insisted on an audience. Later, after her fourth child and only daughter had been born, my mother commented that the little girl was beautiful with eyes so dark they looked black.

Four years after her daughter's birth, when I was a sophomore in high school, Carol divorced her professor husband and moved to the suburbs with her children. Gradually, my father began spending time at her house, sometimes bringing my sister and brothers with him. I refused to participate based on my suspicion that whatever was going on between them had moved beyond the collegial. I accused my father of pretending he had two families. I wanted him to choose between Carol and my mother. But what I really wanted, I see now, was for him to choose my mother, because that meant he would be choosing me.

My mother once gave me an example of the kind of woman who could threaten a marriage. At the time I thought her reference related to fiction, a movie she had seen or a novel she had read. She said that a wife need not fear the extravagant beauty who draws her husband's attention for a time. Worry instead, she told me, about the solicitous "little brown hen" of a woman who befriends your husband.

I wonder now if my mother was thinking about Carol when she made this comment.

I would not characterize Carol as a "little brown hen," though her physical appearance was unremarkable. She had an angular catlike face and a kind of feline alertness. Below average in height, her figure tended toward stoutness. She wore her golden hair, her best feature, in a loose bun held in place with multiple combs.

Carol fit in with her male colleagues, at least in part, as a result of her energy and confidence, and by being more like them in her interests. She fished, hunted, played cards, and smoked the occasional cigar. She could also cook, and like my father, was enthusiastic about food and wine, frequently to excess. They had fun together. Whatever other feelings they shared, friendship sustained them.

My father and Carol eventually became the team my parents once had been, and this must have gnawed at my mother. Perhaps, too, Carol's success as a physician, an ambition my mother had once nurtured, reminded her of a life foregone.

I didn't expect my siblings to raise any objections to our father's relationship with Carol. If they saw an opportunity for fun, and they often did in Carol's home, they did not look beyond that. Challenging our father would not have occurred to them. But I did not understand why my mother remained passive. Her apparent indifference to my father's behavior seemed at the time incomprehensible.

My father had been a force with which my mother contended; she couldn't ignore him, as his personality made that impossible. His focus on her, even when infused with hostility, kept her grounded. Responding to him gave her something to push against, if only from time to time. Without him, she floundered. And despite giving no clue that she cared about his leaving, I wonder now if she felt cast aside.

In *Trauma and Recovery*, Judith Herman warns that the resolution of trauma is never final and recovery is never complete. Post-traumatic symptoms can be revived by other stressful life events. My father's affair may have recalled other betrayals and forced to the surface trauma my mother had been able, for a time, to bury.

My mother remained in our family home, but as surely as my father, she also withdrew.

⚜ ⚜ ⚜

A few years before she died, I asked my mother if she thought she was an alcoholic. I was visiting her in Texas at the time and we had been exploring her history through photographs and stories. As soon as I asked the question, I realized I had wanted to for a long time. By then, she drank infrequently, and when she did, she seemed to have control over her consumption. Nevertheless, whenever I saw my mother with a glass of wine in her hand, I grew agitated, because the image returned me to Pine Street and its desolation.

"I don't know," she said, "but I don't believe alcoholism is a disease. It causes other illnesses." Apparently, my mother viewed her drinking as a choice, something she was able to give up once she decided to do so.

When I first considered her drinking in that light, I struggled with my reaction, imagining that she could have chosen differently. Instead of seeking oblivion, she could have been emotionally present for us, her children. She could have invested in something, in anything, that brought her in touch with the living. I never said this to her—my mother who feared abandonment as a child—but when she deadened herself with alcohol, I felt abandoned.

Bessel van der Kolk, in his research on the nature and effects of trauma, notes that at least half of all traumatized people try to dull their intolerable inner pain with drugs or alcohol. My mother relied on alcohol, but I no longer think of it as a choice. Alcohol abuse was a coping strategy, though that does not lessen the harm.

My mother did not become violent or verbally abusive when she drank. She disappeared, not physically, but in all the ways that mattered to me. Refrains of "Mom, you promised" could sometimes rouse her from her lethargy, but her responses always impressed me as half-hearted.

One evening, my mother attended a performance of my high school's concert choir, in which I sang alto. I had nagged her into coming. As we settled into our positions on stage,

I scanned the audience looking for her. After the concert, I searched the lobby. I found her standing off in a corner, looking unkempt and ill at ease. I had wanted her there, but once I saw her, I wished she had stayed home. On this cold winter night, she wore flip-flops, a choice of attire that, to my mind, revealed a miserable ineptitude.

Odd that I remember this event when my mother's fading away had more painful consequences. But it may be that what stays with me is my embarrassment. That evening I saw my mother as might a stranger.

On a shelf in my office, I have self-help books aimed at the adult children of alcoholics, purchased years ago when I believed my mother was an alcoholic and that her illness could explain our relationship and the troubled Pine Street years. I wanted to find the key to understanding some of the challenges of my adult life—my reluctance to trust others, my sometimes obsessive desire for order and predictability, my perfectionism that interferes with accomplishment, what Tom sometimes bemoans as my negativity but what I think of as a fertile imagination for worst-case scenarios—all of which could be explained if I identified my mother as an alcoholic. I wanted a recognized diagnosis to illuminate the past.

Once, not long before my mother moved from Philadelphia to Texas, I told her that I had never felt I could count on her. In my first semester at Wharton, I took a break from my studies to use the pay phone in Van Pelt Library's basement to call my mother. Whatever possessed me to think she would welcome my candor escapes me now. It may be that thoughts of her imminent departure prompted me toward my disclosure. I might have believed that if I named the problem, she would do something about it. Or perhaps I thought that clarity would strengthen our relationship. She ended the call, not by hanging up on me exactly but with sufficient abruptness that I knew not to pursue the subject. I didn't until years later, and then not in direct conversation with my mother but through my writing.

I cannot say whether my mother was an alcoholic, and I do not think it matters anymore. But I held to my hypothesis that her drinking accounted for her inconstancy, even after she had settled in Texas, and I had no direct evidence that she was abusing alcohol. My anxiety stayed with me. When I tell myself otherwise, I remember my initial reaction to a photograph taken of my mother six years before she died. A family friend arranged for my mother to visit him in Amsterdam, where he had a home. He handled and paid for everything—traveling to Texas so that she would not have to fly overseas alone, organizing itineraries for each day's activities, renting a motorized scooter, as she had trouble walking by then. One last return to Europe, his gift to her, perhaps in gratitude for having welcomed him as a young boy during the times he preferred our home to his own.

In the photograph, my mother sits in her motorized chair, children playing around the splashing fountain behind her. She has a glass of champagne in her right hand and raises it toward our friend. Her smile is sweet and her eyes shine. And I only see that glass.

Other People's Children

In my memories of childhood, I place Lydia, Billy, and Henry together on one side of a divide and myself alone on the other. They formed a band of playmates, sometimes co-conspirators, while I checked myself against a spontaneity and sense of fun they seemed to embody. My position as the oldest probably accounted for some of my seriousness and restraint, traits not unusual in the firstborn, but it went beyond that. And later, as we each navigated adolescence, I remained the outsider, by then most comfortable in that role.

"Every child has a different set of parents," a wise psychologist once told me. Each child presents her parents with her unique personality and potential. They respond accordingly, those responses affected by the child's nature, as well as the parents' capacities as caregivers to that child. Those capacities are influenced by circumstances and by the histories each parent carries into the relationship.

Lydia, Billy, and Henry did not doubt that they were loved. But for reasons I will never fully grasp, I did. And in this instance, feeling matters more than truth.

Growing up, it was to my brother Billy I most often compared myself, perhaps because I sensed that his birth had given my father what he wanted: a son. He was born when I was three and a half years old, enlarging our family to three children. Before I could verbalize the feeling, I recognized Billy as my father's favorite. As for my mother, I could not be sure of her preferences, except to say that by the time I reached my late teens, I understood she felt more at ease with my brothers, and toward the end of her life, she grew closest to Billy.

In a son, a mother does not see a projection of herself, and that simplifies the relationship psychologically. My mother could never fully accept me, at least in part, because she could never fully accept herself. That never seemed at play when it came to her sons.

I competed with Billy in ways I did not with Henry or Lydia. Some of that related to our birth order—I was the oldest child, and he was the first son. We were also similar in our evident ambition to succeed academically, something my father appreciated.

When I was in my early teens, filled with anger looking for an outlet, I used to tell my mother—in a mockery of self-reflection—that I couldn't understand why I so disliked Billy. I always made sure to pose the question when he might hear it, cruelty I still wish I could undo. I wonder why she made no effort to stop me. Perhaps she understood my jealousy, or perhaps she recognized that she was my real target.

Once I entered the University of Pennsylvania, I could have become part of a community, and that would have changed my experience. Instead, I lived a liminal existence as an undergraduate, suspended between engagement with campus life and my desire to be in France, or simply elsewhere. It was a half-life.

Fortunately, in my freshman year I recognized that I could excel academically, so I did. My classes, even those from which

I derived no lasting benefits, grounded me in routine, providing a structure to my days. Summers I headed to France, the friendships I developed there sustaining me during the long academic seasons. Those trips, coupled with living in university housing, removed me from Pine Street, at least physically. And while I was absent, another took my place.

Janet and I had once been best friends, having met when we were eleven and attending the same local middle school. We lived within walking distance of each other and divided our time between her family's house and mine, though I preferred her home.

Her father worked as an engineer and occasionally helped us with more complex school projects. I owe a credible plaster relief map of the United States to his help. Janet's mother taught high school English in the suburbs, and I remember wishing I attended the sleek and polished school. My own mother had stopped working outside of our home when I was too young to remember, so the fact that Janet's mother had somewhere she had to be Mondays through Fridays lent her an aura of mystery and prestige.

Weekends, I sometimes shared dinner with Janet, her parents, and her two older sisters, all of us seated around their large dining room table, a commonplace for them but not something I experienced at Pine Street. Sufficiently impressed by these dinners, I interpreted it as evidence of a stable, close-knit family, ignorant of tension that existed beneath the surface of apparent familial harmony.

I admired Janet's sisters, especially the eldest, already in high school and an aspiring harpist. I appreciated their attention, even when edged with malice. When they insisted on calling me Piglet because of my plumpness, I wanted to see it as a sign of affection. And once, for amusement, they hid a tape recorder in the bathroom next to Janet's bedroom to eavesdrop on our conversation while we got ready for bed. Later, at another family dinner, they played the recording back to us and laughed at the voice I had used when asking to borrow Janet's toothbrush. I didn't know how to tell them that they had proved themselves to be untrustworthy.

Most years, in mid-December, Janet's parents took us to New York City for an afternoon. We would take the train from Philadelphia's 30th Street Station to Penn Station and then walk to Macy's, where I focused on the decorations rather than shopping. As twilight fell, before boarding the train for home, we would have dinner at some inexpensive, noisy place near the train station. I loved walking the New York streets in the cold that tasted like metal, the overcrowded, warm restaurant, and the hot greasy scent of cooking oil.

When Janet visited Pine Street, we sometimes watched *Star Trek* episodes in my parents' bedroom, lounging on the bed. Often enough, my mother joined us there, the three of us lined up with our backs against the headboard. The television show didn't interest my mother, but even then, she preferred her bed to other parts of the house.

Janet and I each nurtured complementary crushes—William Shatner's Captain Kirk for me and Leonard Nimoy's Mr. Spock for Janet. I wonder if Mr. Spock really was her preferred choice, or if my own deprived her of an alternative.

In seventh grade, Janet's and my lives diverged for the first time. I had a boyfriend, though I didn't refer to him as such. Handsome, taller, and physically more developed than the other boys, Ali excelled at kickball and ran like some untamed animal finally set free. Ali was *the* boy, the one against whom the others were compared. He had skin the color of coffee with a touch of cream, prominent ears, a flat nose over full lips. His dark eyes conveyed a kind of reticence, as if he had already learned to withhold aspects of himself. I never learned anything substantive about his home life, except that he lived with his uncle and told us his father was a Samoan prince. No one thought to challenge his assertion. He used to impress us by putting a lighted match out on his forearm. We thought him brave. When I met him, his otherwise perfect skin already bore the scars.

I believed him unattainable, until Janet's middle sister confided that she had kissed him. She was probably amused and intrigued by the fascination he inspired. Her efforts at seduction, albeit limited, seemed an experiment with her own power.

I did not pursue Ali. I would not have known how, but he must have sensed my attraction. The first time he touched me we were at a bowling alley with a group of friends and pretending to concentrate on one of the pinball machines set off in an alcove near the lanes. Ali and I stood close together, aware of each other's proximity. He put his arm around my shoulders, and I felt an electric current flash through my body. I may have stopped breathing, afraid that movement of any kind would break the spell.

In the spring, we started meeting at my house for long walks, usually taking our family's German shepherd with us. I often wanted Janet to come too. She would fall in behind us with our dog, while Ali and I walked ahead holding hands. I'm not sure of my motivation in including Janet, though I do not believe I intended to be mean. I suppose I wanted her to share as much of the experience as possible, even as I knew it belonged to Ali and me.

In junior high school, there were times when I was mean, joining two other girls, more popular than Janet or me, in teasing her. We didn't do it often and always relented soon enough, but I am still ashamed of my behavior. I wanted Abby and Liz to like me and that meant siding with them when they chose to torment Janet. Once, in the lunchroom, when Janet left our table in search of something to drink, they took her sandwich, replacing it with a half-eaten one. When Janet returned, she found what she thought were the remains of her meal on the plate. She didn't say anything, just sat down to eat the leftovers. At that point, Abby or Liz returned her uneaten hoagie, delighted by the joke. I laughed.

Janet suffered from mysterious skin ailments and claimed that she was allergic to the adhesive in Band-Aids, her self-diagnosis likely accurate, but not believable to Abby, Liz, and me. We would occasionally tease her, telling her to "Go wear a Band-Aid," as a way of isolating her. Here, too, I went along.

Sometimes Ali and I walked to the large cemetery that stood a few blocks from my house. To get there, we had to cross SEPTA's 40th Street Trolley Portal, an expanse of cement criss-crossed by steel rails. Designed in the late eighteenth century, Woodland Cemetery's fifty-three acres lay just beyond the trolley terminal, a verdant expanse of winding stone paths and mature trees.

Ali and I had a favorite spot on the grass covering a small hillock, beneath which stood a crypt. Urban traffic and the whine of trolleys lurching into the tunnel surrounded us, but we never heard the sound. I can't recall ever seeing anyone else during our afternoon visits, most often on Saturday. The cemetery's stillness enveloped us as we lay on the grass, turned toward each other. Sometimes Ali cupped my breast while we kissed, and I could feel the warmth of his hand through my shirt and cotton bra. If I had a daughter, I would wish her such sweetness.

Summer arrived and I went off to visit a family friend on her New Jersey farm for a week. The few days away ended my spring with Ali. Our romance could not survive the telling of it. I dropped him with an abruptness I still regret. After that, I saw him only once more in the hallway of our second floor, exiting the bedroom my brothers then shared. Too startled to say anything, I let him pass. Billy and Henry had befriended him, their relationship unfolding without my knowledge. I wonder if Ali sought some kind of solace at Pine Street. I hope he found it.

Once Janet and I both entered the University of Pennsylvania, we drifted apart, preoccupied by different courses of study and different friends, an unsurprising development on the surface. But as our relationship waned, her relationship with my mother intensified.

While at Penn, I was only vaguely aware of Janet's infiltration of Pine Street. She lived there off and on, though I do not remember when or where in the house. I'd stop by and find her there—in the kitchen reaching into the fridge for something to eat, or in a conversation my arrival disrupted.

After my mother died, I invited Janet to the celebration of my mother's life, though I had no connection to her by then, except that we had each figured in the other's past. She had maintained contact with my mother, visiting her on a regular basis during the years they both lived in Texas, Janet in Austin and my mother in nearby Fredericksburg. And she had remained friends with Billy and Lydia, relationships that began at Pine Street and flourished for a time.

Janet brought to the celebration a fourteen-page remembrance of my mother and life in our family home. At her request, Tom read excerpts to the assembled guests. Afterward, she told him that he had made the wrong choices and should have included more of her pages. Her comment amused him and irritated me. Later, when I reviewed the entire piece, I grew more irritated.

The remembrance includes my mother's stories about her childhood and experiences during the war—recollections that Janet recorded and transcribed for a college folklore project in her freshman year. The idea of Janet as the keeper of my mother's history compels me to go through each page, like an editor intent on ensuring accuracy. In a different-colored font, I add my own commentary and correct the errors.

Janet's observations extend to my mother's sewing skills and her wardrobe, especially a beautiful pair of low-heeled pumps in a leather that looked like gunmetal. I remember those shoes—they might have been mine, if I had asked my mother for them. She recalls my mother's preparation of chicken in sour cream and the chocolate cake with coffee-flavored buttercream icing, my two favorite dishes as a child, the cake the one I always chose for my birthday. Apparently, sometimes my mother made it for Janet too, her birthday falling, as mine does, in October.

I learn of summer evenings during college that Janet spent drinking with my mother, vodka and orange juice or vodka and tonic in tumblers of ice, sitting side by side on my mother's bed. Both of them "unhappy," both of them "sad travelers." Overseas, I knew nothing of their shared confidences, but the idea of my mother struggling emotionally does not surprise me.

I wonder if that summer coincided with my father and Carol's trip to England. Lydia, Billy, Henry, and Carol's children all went along. This parody of a family vacation may have been a kind of final insult, in response to which my mother's mask of indifference slipped. I doubt she would have wanted me as a witness to her pain, but, in truth, I did my best to turn away.

I believe Janet hoped to replace me within my family, and especially in relation to my mother. Her desire may have been unconscious and fueled by her own unrecognized wounds. Part of her strategy seemed to involve diminishing me in the eyes of others who knew my family. I noted it in particular at our graduation from Penn, when I tried to say hello to Janet's neighbors—a couple we both knew, and with whom I had a connection through my father, as Dr. Harris had been one of his residents. Dr. Harris and his wife behaved in an aloof, if not cold, manner toward me, in stark contrast to their rapport with Janet.

When Tom and I got married, my mother urged me to invite Janet to the small ceremony and celebration, so I extended an invitation. I wanted to please my mother, and I also thought it might be a way to renew a dormant friendship. Janet never replied, and I interpreted that as definitive evidence she no longer wanted any kind of relationship.

I can dismiss Janet as someone from my past, a person who exited my life. But I can't dismiss my mother's behavior. She treated Janet as though they were intimate. And if that wasn't her intention, then she acted in ways that made it impossible for Janet to believe otherwise.

In being so available to my friend, my mother excluded me from that same intimacy. Yet even though I hold to that opinion, I recognize my own role in increasing the tension between my mother and me, between me and everyone at Pine Street. I withdrew into disapproval, not always verbalized, but apparent in the way I moved through Pine Street as might a reluctant and disdainful visitor.

My mother must have found Janet's devotion affirming and, perhaps at times, healing. Janet loved my mother and their relationship developed without the complications imposed by a shared history.

I returned to France to study in autumn of 1975, the fall semester of my senior year at Penn, finally achieving what I had wanted all along. I lived in Clichy, a near suburb of Paris, with French friends I had met through Didier.

My mother once called my friends' apartment at three in the morning. After passing the phone to me, they hovered in the doorway, worried some catastrophe had befallen my family, but my mother had only confused the six-hour time difference, or hadn't thought about it. I heard multiple voices raised in laughter, what sounded like the noise of a party. I remember thinking my mother might be on her way to being drunk, because of her uncharacteristic animation. Someone called out my name, and for a moment I felt included. "You'll have such a good time here when you get back," my mother said. I wondered what had changed.

While still in Paris, I received a letter from my father. "Your mother has rented your room," I read in his first line. I sat on my bed fingering the single sheet, my father's scrawl covering barely half the page. Given the incomprehensibility of his handwriting, I would have assumed I had misunderstood, except his secretary had provided a typed translation.

My father's announcement communicated more than he perhaps intended. He had separated himself from the life of Pine Street—and from my mother in all but a legal sense—though he kept himself informed of major developments, like my apparent eviction. And yet, I couldn't quite believe my mother had really done it. *Why wouldn't she tell me?* I thought. *Since when is she renting rooms?*

I'd rather have stayed in Paris, but I had to return to Philadelphia to complete my final semester at Penn. I had counted on occupying my bedroom, as I'd always done during winter breaks and parts of each summer. I'd left clothes in the closet, my record collection, posters on the walls. I'd thought of that particular room as mine and believed my mother would await my homecoming, or at least keep a place for me in the house.

In December, when I returned from France, I found my bedroom vacant, though the rumpled, sour-smelling bed linens revealed this to be a recent development. *She didn't even change the sheets*, I remember thinking. *So much for welcome home.*

By then, my brother Henry lived with my father in the apartment he had rented in the suburbs. Henry and I had learned to ignore each other, an approach made easier by the six years that separated us. I didn't know anything about his life then, and whatever opinions I held of his behavior and prospects were negative.

My brother Billy had started his freshman year at Penn while I was still in Paris. He had planned to live in university housing with his friend John, but John had missed the deadline to submit the appropriate paperwork. Rather than live with some stranger randomly assigned as a roommate, my brother decided to stay at Pine Street. He and John took over Granny's old apartment, along with Billy's bedroom. A door from Billy's room connected to the hallway and the second-floor interior entrance to the apartment. My brother's bedroom and the apartment became a kind of male-dominated compound, one I avoided.

My sister, Lydia, also studying at Penn, still occupied her bedroom on Pine Street's third floor. A red sweater, one I had purchased in Paris, provides the only reason I remember her whereabouts from that time. I never loaned clothes to her and would not have let her borrow my sweater, so she took it without asking.

One afternoon, not long after my return from France, I found Lydia in my mother's bedroom, sitting on the bed, both of them smoking. The ash from Lydia's cigarette fell on the sweater and burned a large hole. I do not remember what I said, though I expect both my mother and sister found my anger exaggerated. It was just a piece of clothing to them, nothing to make a fuss about, but it was more than that to me. Wearing the sweater reminded me of Paris and my time there, an interval during which I'd felt like I belonged within a world I admired.

I met Rick just before departing for France. Though immediately attracted to him, I did not expect anything to come of our weekend's flirtation, but we started dating after my return to Pine Street. Our relationship continued for about six months and, ultimately, did not encourage the best in either one of us.

Some of what drew me to Rick, I see now, was that I believed associating with him made me more interesting. I wouldn't call him a rebel or an iconoclast, but when he straddled his motorcycle in his black leather jacket and pants, he looked the part.

He knew my brothers and sister, my parents too, though our respective families had lost touch over the years. Our fathers, both surgeons, had been medical school classmates. The apparent ease Rick felt at Pine Street, and with my family, appealed to me too. Perhaps I thought he would bring us closer.

Rick never spent the night in my room, though I doubt my mother would have raised any questions about it. And my father, who might have asked some questions, wasn't around. Rick and I did, however, retreat to my bedroom for sex. Our sexual encounters were boisterous enough that the privacy I had assumed we enjoyed proved to be an illusion.

I might have remained ignorant but for my mother. I had come into her bedroom, perhaps to ask a question or merely to confirm her location. She lay in bed, Billy beside her, the two of them watching television. She said something about hearing everything that went on in my bedroom. I remember my embarrassment, made worse by my brother's presence. I wished she would just keep her mouth shut.

It strikes me now that my discomfort might have surprised her. Or perhaps making me uncomfortable had been her intent. She may have found it all amusing—evidence that her buttoned-up daughter could behave with such abandon.

Once, when my deteriorating mattress started to sprout metal wires that drew blood, I asked Lydia if Rick and I could use her bed. Or, more likely, informed her that I was taking over her room and waited for an objection, completely warranted, that never came. I look back on that incident and think about how I trampled on whatever boundaries my sister hoped to maintain, scarce as they were at Pine Street.

One summer evening, Rick and I sit at the picnic table in the kitchen. Rick says something about my scaring him, without clarifying what he means. I don't ask. I have a fleeting thought about not wanting to be involved with a man I can intimidate. Rick has seen glimpses of my anger toward my mother, so this may be his frame of reference. I couldn't have told him why she could inspire such fury; I didn't know myself.

He tells me that he wants to end our relationship. I will be the outsider again and lose whatever sense of belonging being with him gave me. I believe that by sheer force of will, I can make him stay.

A couple of weeks later, my mother confronts me about what I said to Rick: "Did you really tell him you would not let him leave you?" the contempt in her voice unmistakable. *How do you know about that?* I think, too shocked to respond.

"How can a man sleep with you and then leave you?" she asks, her question a taunt, for which I have no answer.

It has taken me a long time to understand that her question didn't really have anything to do with me. Her question had to do with her faith in a woman's power to control a man with sex. And, also, her fear. Fear of what happens when a woman loses that control. That said, even after all of these years, I still react physically to the memory of that encounter with my mother, my chest growing tight.

I soon guessed how my mother had learned of my conversation with Rick. He had shared the details of our breakup with his friend Daniel, who then relayed it all to my mother. The idea that I had been the subject of gossip and ridicule, and that my mother had participated, upset me as much as anything she said.

That summer after the end of my relationship with Rick proved to be a low point in my self-esteem. After graduating from Penn, I landed a job in market research for a Philadelphia-based advertising firm, but it did not pay me enough to rent my own apartment. I felt trapped at Pine Street. The social life I had enjoyed as a result of dating Rick evaporated, leaving me feeling isolated.

During this distressing time, emotional support came from two unlikely sources. I did not know Billy's friend John other than to recognize his closeness to my brother. But, one day, when he encountered me by chance in the house, he stopped me. He put his hand on my shoulder and in a gentle voice said that he hoped I would be happy, because I deserved to be.

Billy also surprised me, revealing a gallantry I had not expected. Before Rick ended our relationship, I had purchased tickets for us to see *Equus*, a play that had received excellent reviews in New York and was to begin a series of performances in Philadelphia. In an effort to maintain contact with Rick, I invited him to come to the play with me. He accepted the invitation, but then on the day of the performance failed to appear. Without me asking, Billy accompanied me.

I made one last effort to revive my relationship with Rick a few weeks later. I went to visit him in the apartment he shared with another man in the suburbs, not someone I had ever met. Rick and I ended up in bed, and then I ended up in the apartment's kitchen wearing only a bathrobe. Rick had told me that if his roommate returned while we were together, I should not introduce myself. I did not challenge his explanation that he didn't want to answer any questions about me, even though I sensed the lie. I suspected that this roommate would know exactly who I was, having heard whatever stories Rick had told about me and our breakup. When his roommate arrived at the apartment, Rick behaved as though I were not seated there in the kitchen, leaving this stranger and me to stare at each other for a few awkward moments. I remember wanting to rebel and tell this man my name, but I didn't. Even as I let the silence accumulate, I resolved to never behave in that way again. No man would ever make me invisible.

Daniel and my sister have different interpretations of how he came to occupy my room while I was in Paris. From his perspective, my mother's offer of the room was an act of kindness during a time when he was floundering professionally and personally. From Lydia's point of view, our mother's decision represented a choice of Daniel over her. She and Daniel had dated briefly that summer, and though their tentative romance had ended amicably, my sister did not want him living at Pine Street.

Whenever I think of my mother's behavior, I want to ask her what she was thinking, though it never occurred to me to do so at the time. I understand my sister's indignation, because I shared it. Lydia's distress should have deterred our mother from inviting Daniel into our home. And even if she were reluctant to let my sister's objections curb her own generous impulse, why didn't she demonstrate any concern for Lydia's feelings, for my own?

I see now that my mother may have been incapable of that kind of reasoning. Whatever haunted her—multiple past traumas, the unraveling of her marriage, other harm I know nothing about—compromised her judgment. Her choices seemed to be driven by those threats, so that she gave my room to Daniel, not so much to help him but in response to some unrecognized need of her own.

My mother and Daniel's friendship, begun that autumn, lasted until her death, and was, for both of them, an instance of grace.

She referred to Daniel as her best friend, and though I cannot remember when she started calling him that, I do remember how hearing that characterization rankled me. Their age difference struck me as incompatible with friendship, certainly when Daniel was in his mid-twenties and my mother in her early fifties. That Daniel seemed to have shifted his attention from my sister to my mother troubled me. That she seemed to cultivate his attention made me angry.

I found their relationship unseemly, as if my mother had trespassed to claim a friendship that belonged to my sister. A not-so-subtle competition may have been underway, my mother enjoying the admiration of a much younger man at my sister's expense. I sympathized with my sister, but my grievance had more to do with my own feelings of displacement. I resented my mother and Daniel's easy rapport, resented the secrets they shared. Their closeness served to magnify the gulf between my mother and me.

Once, during my final months at Pine Street, I found myself in the living room with Daniel, my mother, and a monkey. I consider that description and want to add, *No, I'm not kidding*. At the time, Daniel worked in a laboratory that used small primates in some of its research. One of the young monkeys had been orphaned, and he was raising her before returning her to the colony.

Sarah, the name Daniel had given the monkey, clung to his thick reddish-brown hair, a color similar to her fur, so that she remained largely hidden unless she moved. Sometimes her long tail dangled at his shoulder, revealing her presence. My mother relished imagining how strangers would respond to Sarah's sudden appearance, erupting into distinctive *hee-hee-hee* sounds, her version of laughter, but one that never struck me as genuine. I didn't find any of this amusing. Instead, I wondered what happened when Sarah had to urinate or defecate. Did she leave the nest Daniel's hair provided? I pondered this problem as I sat on the other side of the large teak table watching my mother and Daniel on the couch. They were drinking cocktails.

At one point, Sarah leapt from Daniel's head directly into a martini glass. My mother found this hilarious, while I had to suppress the urge to grab the monkey and hurl her across the room. I remember thinking that would surely get my mother's attention.

Did that desire fuel my rage? In retrospect, it seems so. I longed for my mother to *attend* to me—by giving me her care and consideration, by being present for me in the ways she seemed to be for others. I'd wanted that since our beginning.

❖ ❖ ❖

I lived at Pine Street during my last semester at Penn and for another eight months, commuting to work by bus. As soon as I secured another job that paid me more, I found my own apartment, a sublet crowded with the official renter's furniture and books. Her clothes, holding faint traces of rose and jasmine, still hung in the bedroom closet. But none of that mattered. Each time I opened the door, a feeling of calm settled over me. That small one-bedroom apartment, separate from Pine Street, felt like my home, or at least the promise of home.

I still returned to Pine Street, but I never slept there again. Sometimes worry prompted my visit, my imagination for disaster vivid. One day I couldn't reach my mother on the phone, even though I knew she had to be in the house, as she rarely left. My stomach knotted with each unanswered call, as I envisioned her unconscious on the floor. No longer able to cope with my anxiety, agitation propelled me to West Philadelphia. I found my mother sitting in the living room, encircled by the silvery smoke of her Benson and Hedges Menthol 100.

"I've been calling, why didn't you answer the phone?" I asked.

"Oh, I didn't hear it."

I didn't believe her. She just didn't want to be bothered.

Frustrated, I turned around and walked out the door.

On another occasion, I stopped by Pine Street and found the debris of a raucous party Billy had thrown the night before. I doubt he knew all of the guests; strangers showed up for what was then referred to as a "blowout." Empty bottles and discarded plastic cups littered the dirty wooden floor. The place reeked of stale beer and cigarettes. Discarded in a corner of the living room, I found one of our Eames chairs—its elegant curves had made it seem alive—shattered.

I doubt I talked to my mother that day, not wanting to linger in a place increasingly alien. Had I looked for her, I expect I would have found her in her bedroom. I'd once viewed that place as her realm; it's where everyone went to speak to her. From the confines of her bed, she had offered stories, sometimes advice. But the room had become something else. A tomb.

My mother occupied the left side of the bed; the right belonged to whomever wished to linger with her. Pillows were pulled out, the bedspread rumpled. She changed the sheets when food stains, dog hair—our German shepherd slept at the foot of the bed—and other grime accumulated to more than she wished to tolerate.

One of my last images of that room centers on the plastic pitcher my mother kept on the shelf above the fireplace. The house's two bathrooms, one on the third floor and the other on the first, stood at a distance from her second-floor room. During the night, urinating in the plastic pitcher was more convenient. But she didn't empty it first thing in the morning. She let the urine accumulate until the container couldn't hold any more.

I did not witness the worst of my mother's depression and alcohol abuse. I had moved out of Pine Street in early spring of 1977. Sometimes I wonder if my presence, like my father's before me, would have been a deterrent to my mother's slide toward insensibility. Suggesting that feels like self-aggrandizement, but I always believed my mother made more of an effort at self-control around me.

Daniel and I talked recently about the two years between my moving out and my father's death, a time he described as "really dark" for my mother. Looking back, I think Billy's absence also contributed to her decline. He departed Pine Street to spend his junior year in Edinburgh the autumn after my move, so he also escaped. After he left, other people's children filled the house.

During this time, Daniel once asked my mother if she wanted to die, her drinking and despondency prompting his question, and she admitted that she did. I wonder if acknowledging her misery to Daniel blunted it. Or did something else keep my mother among the living? She is the only one who can answer that question. That said, I do not believe my mother would have committed suicide, though had she continued to abuse alcohol, the end result might have been the same.

My mother possessed an inner core of strength that kept her from complete self-destruction. She may have been born with it, or it may have been forged by her traumatic past, like a natural diamond created by intense heat and pressure.

My father's sudden death sobered her, figuratively and literally. She stopped drinking, if only for a time, and that pause allowed her to recover parts of herself. She told me once that she refused to fall apart after he died, because so many expected her to do so. Concern for us, my brothers, my sister, and me, may also have strengthened her resolve, though even as I write that, I recognize in my hypothesis an element of wishful thinking. Losing her would have made us orphans, but that was not her primary concern. She feared losing herself.

Powers of Attraction

My parents saw each other for the last time on a late spring day in 1979. My father had stopped by Pine Street on his way to New Orleans, where he was to attend the annual meeting of the American Association of Tissue Banks, an organization he had helped create.

I wonder what would have happened if either one of them had recognized the finality of my father's visit. What might have been different? Would anything have been resolved or clarified?

I stood on the periphery of their relationship—all children do where their parents are concerned—even though I felt the aftershocks. I still do.

My father would have greeted my mother when he arrived, "Lodestone, where are you?" I see him standing just inside the door, his gaze directed up the stairs to the second floor. He keeps calling as he climbs, turning the nickname into an incantation.

Growing up, I cringed whenever I heard my father call my mother Lodestone, because it made me think of a dead weight, a burden against which you would struggle. When I asked my mother about the name, she explained that a lodestone was a magnetic mineral, believed by some to possess magical qualities of attraction. I see some truth in both interpretations.

My father finds my mother in the bedroom they once shared. She sits on the bed, her back supported by pillows arrayed in front of the headboard, her legs rigid in a position that always looked uncomfortable to me but suited her joints' hypermobility. She might be reading or watching television, or perhaps doing both and focusing on neither. Depending on the time of day and her mood, a glass of Gallo Chianti waits on the table next to the bed. She bought the wine by the gallon and kept it at the bottom of the refrigerator, serving it in containers that had once held Breakstone's sour cream. I suspect she preferred her makeshift wine glass to a traditional goblet for its durability and larger capacity. And, in any case, if any crystal still survived somewhere in the house, it had been forgotten.

Later, when my mother thought about that day, she said that she had been struck by how handsome my father had looked in his blue pinstripe suit. She had felt a sudden urge to touch his cheek but had not acted upon it. Perhaps some buried tenderness remained, though he would have been startled by its expression.

A few days into his trip, he fell ill and was admitted to New Orleans Baptist Hospital. His fever, nausea, and vomiting led doctors initially to suspect Rocky Mountain spotted fever, because he had been hunting in an affected area and the symptoms matched. When my mother heard the diagnosis, she said, "Leave it to your father to catch something bizarre." I think she meant to comment on his originality.

But the physicians misdiagnosed him. My father had fulminant hepatitis, acute liver failure, brought on by hepatitis B. I would learn later that he had contracted the virus while operating on an infected patient, who, at the time of surgery, had been asymptomatic. My father wore latex gloves, so either the glove had an indiscernible flaw or he created a pinprick hole while suturing. That opening, along with a wound on his hand (from a laser procedure, experimental at the time, to remove a mole) combined to infect him. The disease progressed aggressively to destroy my father's liver, killing him within days of diagnosis.

I spoke to him shortly after he had been hospitalized, not realizing it would be the last time. I almost didn't make the call, because I'd assumed he would recover and return soon—I thought him indestructible. And he had always insisted the phone be used only to convey information as succinctly as possible, not for conversation. "Get off the phone," he'd say upon arriving home if one of us seemed engaged in idle chatter. I kept my message brief: I was thinking of him and would see him when he got back. "Bye, baby," he said. I thought how gentle and subdued his voice, tender in a way I had never heard.

My father had just turned fifty-six. I was twenty-four. We had seemed on the threshold of a greater ease with each other, something that had eluded us in the too few years we had together.

My father died on a Sunday, and I went back to work the next day, not intending to tell anyone what had happened. My supervisor found me standing in the hallway of the bank's credit department. With a grin, he asked, "So, what did *you* do this weekend?" I didn't know what to tell him. *My father died*, screamed through my skull. *Oh nothing*, occurred to me as a response, but lying felt impossible. I answered quietly, "My father died." It was like pouring a bucket of water on him. He sputtered, looked alarmed, and then tried to regain his composure. "Why are you at work?" he stammered. *Because being elsewhere was too awful*, I thought, but I didn't say that. Instead, I said, "Because my father would have wanted me to be here. I have work to do." I have no idea what my father would have wanted, except to be alive.

When I consider my parents' marriage, I am sometimes reminded of a poem by Sharon Olds, "I Go Back to May 1937." Olds envisions stopping her parents before they wed. They are wrong for each other, she tells us, and they will do things to each other they cannot imagine ever doing.

My parents hurt each other in ways they could not have foreseen and made their children collateral damage. Unlike the poet's parents, however, mine seemed uniquely suited to each other—their coupling inevitable and full of promise. But I now see that what drew them together is also what ultimately divided them.

"He zeroed in on me practically right away," my mother said of their first meeting. My parents worked at the same hospital, my father as a fourth-year medical student and my mother with her degree already in hand. She taught him how to suture a wound, demonstrating the correct 90-degree angle for entering and exiting the skin, the way that technique ensures proper alignment of the skin's edges to minimize scarring. There's some irony in the nature of their earliest collaboration. Trauma, effectively dealt with here, emerged as a motif in their marriage.

My mother's assurance and skill impressed my father, along with her blonde beauty. Within his medical school class of 140, there were only three women. And here before him stood this accomplished and confident doctor. Lesser men might have resented her presence in a male-dominated profession; my father didn't.

His wit and sense of humor seduced her initially, and his attentiveness and persistence no doubt flattered her. Always competitive, once he set his hopes on my mother, I doubt she long resisted. I recall what he told me years later about how he became chief of plastic surgery, when he was not the favored candidate. Other surgeons possessed greater seniority and national visibility, as well as more conventional leadership styles. He won the position by outproducing his rivals in both research and clinical work.

My father possessed a vitality that felt, at its best, like an invigorating current of energy. If I arrived at his offices at the University of Pennsylvania Hospital when he was in surgery or on rounds seeing patients, I sometimes waited for his return. I heard him first, calling out to a secretary or colleague, his Southern drawl teasing, a sound that slid easily into laughter. He walked in at his habitually brisk pace, his residents hurrying to catch up. It proved impossible not to smile at his approach. His presence animated everyone around him.

For a time, he animated my mother, or so it seems to me now. Depression did not yet haunt her days when they first met, though she may have sensed the presence of that specter. Being the focal point of my father's boundless energy must have lifted her spirits.

After my father died, my mother told me that during the early years of their marriage he had carried a photograph of her breasts in his wallet. Just her breasts. Perhaps he had taken a nude shot of her from the waist up and then discarded what failed to interest him. Having set his sights on plastic and reconstructive surgery, he may have been looking for a model.

Had I asked about her reaction, she would have no doubt told me that her breasts *had been lovely*, high and full with a generous separation between them. She viewed my father's keepsake as a kind of homage.

My mother's anecdote surprised, even disturbed, me at first.

I can see my father's behavior as objectifying her; from my current vantage point, that's obvious. If he, in fact, took a photograph of her nude body and then cut away what didn't capture his attention, there's an element of violence, if subtle. But the truth is that I have no idea what motivated him. He admired my mother's figure—especially her breasts. He found her beautiful, and she knew it.

I have only two photographs of my parents together, the first taken before they married. They wear formal attire: my father a tuxedo, my mother a strapless black beaded gown. I believe the occasion was the medical school's interfraternity ball, an event my father's yearbook described as "the highlight of the medical school social season." My father has given my mother a corsage; the white flowers cascade from where she's pinned it at her waistband. She never thought she photographed well, but this image shows them both to fine advantage. They make a stunning couple. *Look at us*, her wide grin suggests, *we're a team, and unbeatable*.

On my dresser sits the second photograph, the lone surviving image from their wedding day. I found it in a box crowded with photos my mother kept in her closet.

When I asked her to let me have the photo, she resisted. "It's a terrible picture of me."

"But I like it. You look so happy," I told her.

"We *were* happy."

My parents married in June 1953 at the First Presbyterian Church of Valdosta, Georgia, the town in which my father grew up. Neither of them attended church, but they accommodated my paternal grandmother's wishes that a minister perform the service. Guests were few, though I assume my father's aunt, uncle, and cousins attended, as they lived nearby. My mother's parents, both in Philadelphia by then, did not see their only child marry. My mother would not have cared about their absence, nor would she have invested the event with undue importance. She viewed her wedding ceremony, however pleasant, as a necessary step to launch the marriage, not as an occasion to celebrate.

In the photograph, they are exiting a door marked "Pastor's Study." A guest has just thrown rice. The flying grains sparkle as though on fire. Nearby, white azaleas catch the sunlight. My father wears a light gray suit, the middle button closed at his slim waist, a white shirt and patterned tie, a white carnation affixed to his lapel. My mother's corsage, the color of strawberries, matches the trim of her black knit suit, an outfit chosen as elegant and more practical than a wedding gown. She's swept her blonde hair up into a French twist under a delicate cap she wears like a crown.

The camera has caught my parents mid-step. My father's left arm, entwined with my mother's right, rests on her steady forearm. Their smiles are exuberant, joy propelling them forward.

My father once told me that he thought he'd found in my mother another maverick. I remember thinking it a compelling characterization of my independent and unconventional parents. They seemed to possess such strong inner compasses that they needed no guidance or approval from anyone else.

In addition to describing a *maverick* as someone not bound by traditional authority or social mores, the dictionary offers another meaning, one that seems equally apt, as if my father had sensed some deeper connection. A *maverick* can also refer to a calf that has become separated from its mother.

My parents both suffered from troubled maternal relationships. That fracturing of what is arguably a child's most important bond had lasting detrimental effects. Though they would not have thought of themselves in this way, my parents shared similar wounds, and that may have contributed to their mutual attraction. But they could not help each other heal. Their unattended injuries eventually infected their marriage.

When my father was five, his father died, leaving his mother to raise him, but without adequate financial resources. She reluctantly left Mississippi to return to her widowed mother's home in Georgia. I would like to believe she found comfort in the presence of her only child, my father, the physical reminder of her husband, but I fear he represented more burden than balm, and in the knowing way of even the youngest children, he would have sensed her reticence.

My great-grandmother disliked my father; it's all I know of her. I envision her stern and disapproving, resentful of the ways in which a little boy, any little boy, disrupted the order of her household. My father found himself isolated and dependent on two women, one buried in her own unhappiness and the other hostile.

A photograph I can no longer find, but remember with a surprising clarity, reveals my father on the stone stoop of what I take to be his grandmother's house. He is nine or ten, delicate with a young boy's grace. He squints into the bright Georgia sunshine. He kneels on one knee, probably to draw closer to his dog, Stafford. His stance allows him to put his arm around the terrier's shoulders, as if presenting his best friend. What looks like a grin in the dog's expression matches my father's. They are a unit, these two, the boy and his dog.

One summer, while my father was away at Boy Scout camp, his grandmother got rid of Stafford. "Out of spite," my mother told me. She didn't clarify what "getting rid of" entailed. Was Stafford put down, given away?

I picture my father returning home, buoyed by the progress he's made toward becoming an Eagle Scout, the highest honor awarded to scouts and achieved by very few. The afternoon is hot, everything slowed down in submission to the heat. The humidity has made the screen door at the back of the house swell, so my father has to yank on the handle to open it. As he steps into the empty kitchen, he doesn't look for his grandmother or mother. He only wants to see Stafford, surprised not to have already found him outside sleeping in the shade of a tree or in the shadow of the house, anywhere it's cool. *Stafford, I'm back—here, boy!* Any minute, he thinks, he'll hear the scrape of the dog's claws on the wooden floor, see him careening around the corner. He'll roll on the grass with him, play fetch (even though Stafford tends to lie down with the ball between his paws, rather than bring it back). He yearns for the feel of his dog under his hands, that glimpse of what looks like ecstasy on Stafford's face when he rubs his belly. Maybe he can find a treat in the kitchen for him, since no one is around to object.

He is met with an empty silence.

Who tells him Stafford is gone? His mother? His grandmother? Does it matter?

Having loved dogs, the worst thing might not be losing them. The worst thing would be not knowing their fates, because I would imagine them suffering somewhere I couldn't reach them. I am sure my father never forgave his grandmother, and likely held his own mother responsible as well. I know this because I would never have forgiven them.

I do not believe my father had anyone he could trust as a child. I doubt he considered the psychological legacy of that kind of insecurity, nor the implications of having a compromised relationship with women from a very young age. I can't analyze the effects of my father's early mistreatment, but it seemed to me that my mother at times unleashed some buried hurt in him, and when he felt threatened, he could respond with cruelty.

I was born sixteen months after my parents married. My sister and brothers followed in quick succession. Beyond assisting my father for a few years in his research, my mother never returned to medicine, so our beginnings seeded an ending. She didn't look at it that way, or resent the sacrifice of her career, but having four children in six years took her away from the field. And, in any case, she'd already encountered problems in having her Austrian credentials recognized in the United States.

Sometimes I wonder how my parents' relationship would have changed had my mother been able to practice medicine.

She liked the intellectual stimulation the field offered, but being a doctor was not essential to her, not in the way being a surgeon felt to my father. Still, while I was in my teens, she attempted to pass the medical board exams so that she could complete a residency and obtain her license.

Afternoons when I returned to the house, I'd find her surrounded by medical texts. She used a highlighter and a plastic ruler to mark passages she found relevant, entire pages painted in yellow. I hoped she would pass, not because I thought she'd be an excellent doctor, though I did, but because I wanted her to have something at which she excelled that had nothing to do with my father. Whatever happened between them, and however it made them feel about themselves, he had medicine, a world in which his mastery had earned him respect and renown, even love.

My mother came within a few points of succeeding on each of her two attempts at the medical boards. She never tried again.

"We were happy for many years," my mother said.

"For how long?" I persisted. I wanted a chronology, in which I might place myself.

"Oh, at least ten years."

That makes sense to me, because I do not remember their contentment, only its absence.

Once, when I was around nine or ten, I came upon my mother in the laundry room at the back of the house. She had decided to get rid of some dishes.

"Here, break one," she invited me.

I wanted to preserve the fragile eggcup she had placed in my hand.

"But, Mom, why are you breaking the dishes?"

"Because it feels great," she said.

She kept smashing them against the laundry room's concrete floor. The shattering reverberated in the relatively empty space. I felt uneasy, unsure why she had embarked on this destruction. It wasn't like we had extra dishes, and in any case, I'd never known her to take on this kind of housecleaning. That kind of organizing belonged to other families, orchestrated by other mothers. And without the broken porcelain.

I wanted to be encouraged by her burst of energy, but her behavior felt dangerous, a warning that more than dishes would prove to be breakable.

Whenever I try to identify the beginning of what I experienced as the war between my parents, my search leads me to Erika. She acted as an unknowing catalyst, igniting something between my parents that flared out of control.

Years after my father had died, my mother still remembered his initial description of Erika. He told her that a German woman (Erika was born in Germany but had settled in the United States) had come to him as a prospective patient, and that she reminded him of how beautiful he imagined my mother had been in Vienna.

The comparison alarmed my mother, far more than my father's apparent fascination. She understood imagination's power. How could she compete with a more youthful and idealized version of herself?

My mother told me once that she had always believed my father remained irresistibly drawn to her. She felt confident of her hold on him. I don't remember if *hold* was the word she used, but it seems fitting. Erika introduced some new variable my mother wasn't sure how to manage, and for the first time in her life, she was jealous of another woman.

I have a few photographs of my mother from that time, and they include some of the most flattering images I have ever seen. In one photo, she sits with her legs crossed, leaning forward and looking toward whoever has drawn her attention, a pensive expression on her face. Her long legs are clad in sheer black textured stockings; her honey-colored arms are bare. A silver sheath drapes her body's soft curves, the fabric's texture reminiscent of a knight's mail.

Another photo from that evening presents a close-up of my mother's face. Perhaps the photographer, most likely my father, wished to capture what I see. Her blonde hair, short during those few years, is swept back, highlighting her high forehead and the angles of her cheekbones. She wears pale lipstick on her wide mouth, dark eyeliner, black mascara to separate each long lash. She holds her mouth slightly open as though she is about to say something. Her eyes, changeable, but here a clear green, look toward the photographer, her gaze searching. *What a stunning woman*, I want to say now. *Whatever competition is underway here, she is winning*.

In summer, instead of the conventional black tank suit, my mother wore a bikini—a bright orange one that looked like suede. We belonged to a swim club, newly established some eight blocks from where we lived. In her early forties, my mother could pull off the style when most of her contemporaries were well-advised to avoid it. But at age twelve, I didn't appreciate her daring. Whenever she emerged from the pool, water droplets sticking to her sun-bronzed body, her breasts rounded over the cups of her bikini top, I wanted her to cover up with a towel. I couldn't see her then as a woman in her prime; I wanted her to look like the other mothers. I wanted her to behave like the other mothers by bringing Tupperware containers of food and keeping extra towels and suntan lotion on hand. But her children were the least of her concerns. We were not neglected in any obvious way, but I felt as if she had stopped seeing me.

Erika, by capturing the attention of both of my parents, occupied the place I should have held as the oldest daughter at the onset of puberty. I might have been the one to remind my parents of my mother's youth. Instead, I bumbled through this transition into adolescence alone, but I wonder how it would have been different if either of my parents had noticed me as I waited on the threshold.

My parents entertained more during those years, parties that blur one into the other. My memories of them exist as shards of glass, a shattered mirror through which I see only distorted images. Too much noise, as everyone grows increasingly drunk, barking laughter that never sounds like happiness. The smell of cigarette smoke, spilled wine, leftover food congealing on the crowded table.

A bullet hole in the living room floor punctuates what I remember of the charged intensity surrounding my parents. I cannot recall if I witnessed the gun's firing, but I may be blocking that memory. If I'd been in the room, I would have been terrified and unable to intervene.

Unexpected and loud noises agitate me to this day. I startle and then need a few minutes to recover my calm. I wonder if my reaction is related to the sound of that gun, my body recalling something my mind has forgotten. Or perhaps my body remembers something that doesn't even belong to me but originated with someone else. My mother or maybe my grandmother?

My mother enjoyed bragging about my father's skilled marksmanship and her steady nerves, so I know the story of how my father stood on a chair and fired a revolver between her spread fingers planted on the wooden floor. A party trick to entertain the assembled guests. And now, decades later, I want to scream at them. *What kind of insanity prompted you to take such a risk?* Yet, if I had the chance to revisit the incident with my mother, I'm not convinced she wouldn't still defend it, insisting once again that my father was an excellent shot.

The demonstration would have been my mother's idea, because my father didn't boast about any of his skills. He liked confounding people by overturning their expectations. He also respected gun safety and would not have retrieved the revolver for amusement. But, like my mother, he'd probably consumed enough alcohol to impair his judgment. Thankfully, the booze didn't affect his aim.

On another evening, also animated by too much alcohol, my parents started arguing on the way home from someone else's party. My mother was so angry she refused to come into the house, telling my father she'd sleep in the car. He left her there and went to bed. Later, as the night grew colder, she changed her mind, but my father had already locked the doors. I don't know what awakened me—the banging on the door, my father's angry voice as he descended the stairs, or my mother's shrill response.

Much as I wanted to, I couldn't ignore my parents' argument; I had to go downstairs. I remember being alone, but my brother Billy told me recently that he was there too, though I cannot place him in the foyer that night. The truth is I cannot paint a portrait of my brothers' and sister's lives then. I don't know how they coped. Each of us retreated into our individual foxholes.

A neighbor, fearing violence, had called the police, and an officer appeared at the door. Our German shepherd, always protective, lunged for him. The officer assumed one of my parents had set Bruce upon him and in response called for assistance. The officer-in-distress signal brought more policemen to the door. One officer drew his gun and threatened to shoot Bruce if my mother didn't get him under control. She shielded him with her body, pleading, "Don't shoot him, he's my only friend."

The police, now angry themselves, would not accept my parents' assurances that their argument was over, that they would remain calm. Two officers dragged my father out the door and down the steep stone steps to their waiting car. *He has no shoes. What about his shoes?* I thought. The next day when he returned home, his hands and neck were bruised and one eye blackened.

At the time, my father was the designated surgeon for the city's police department. My brother told me that the officers discovered this once my father was in custody. An officer was about to summon the department's surgeon to treat my father's injuries, only to be told that their surgeon was already present, behind bars.

My father contemplated filing a lawsuit against the police department, but neither he nor the department wanted the publicity, so they let the matter drop.

My parents' argument attracted news coverage from the local paper—and, to me, roughly thirteen at the time, that seemed the worst of it. The local paper characterized the incident as a "domestic dispute." Even our dog was mentioned. Name, age, everything.

I blamed our neighbor for the police presence and the resulting exposure. My mother defended her, telling me that calling the police, even if it had been unnecessary, required courage. Too few people involve themselves, my mother insisted. And that was the problem, I didn't want anyone else involved. Of course, I wanted my parents to stop fighting, but if they wouldn't, I wanted their battles to remain private.

When I returned to school right after the article had appeared, I studied the faces of my classmates and teachers, fearful I'd see shock or pity there, not sure which reaction would have upset me more.

My mother once told me that her parents' relationship had made her feel tainted. I'd felt the same way about my father and her. Their behavior humiliated me, as if it revealed some terrible familial flaw.

Sometime after the incident involving the police—it could have been a matter of weeks or months—my parents had the worst of their fights. According to my mother, she baited my father by destroying a gift he had given her. Erika had helped him select the luxury handbag. Perhaps her involvement angered my mother. Or, perhaps, she just wanted to hurt my father.

I remember the dark brown bag, dressy, made of some exotic leather, crocodile. The purse seemed impractical to me because of its formality and small size, not something I could see my mother using. But it was expensive. Once she'd ruined it, she knew my father would be furious.

I was not a witness to my father's rage, but I was there the next day.

I found them in the bedroom in the late morning, a time I would not have expected to see my father at home. The weather must have been balmy, because the window was open, and sunlight trembled in patterns on the wooden floor. My mother was sitting on the bed, her legs straight in front of her. She leaned forward, her hands holding the sides of her knees, while my father injected an analgesic around her spine. During the fight, I would learn later, he'd shoved her against the stairs and the blow had fractured some of her vertebrae. There would have been bruising, but I didn't notice it. I focused on my father's hand. I can still see his fingers spreading the skin around each vertebra to hold it taut. His nimble white hand against her pale back.

No one spoke.

My stomach knotted.

I felt most sorry for my father, not because he was the injured party. I understood that he had hurt my mother, if not the extent of her injuries. But he seemed so lost, as if he had arrived somewhere he no longer recognized himself. I see this as another kind of displacement, my father separated from what he'd understood as his code of behavior. He believed, and had taught us, that a man should never strike a woman. His failure to honor his own principles no doubt tormented him.

Much later, my mother told me that my father had asked her to forgive him. He said he wanted to rebuild their marriage and asked if she would try. She told me she had agreed, but in her heart knew it was impossible, because he would never forgive her for being a witness to his worst instincts. She may have been right, but I wish she had allowed herself to be less certain and more open to possibility. And I wonder if my father sensed her heart's closing.

My parents' marriage didn't shatter from the impact of one violent event, but that incident eroded their faith in each other. It seems to me that they lost whatever capacity they each possessed to inspire the best in the other. Instead of sustaining them, as it once did, their union diminished them both.

I don't remember when my father started talking about divorce, not to my mother as far as I know, but to the rest of us. Maybe he didn't speak to my mother because doing so would have made divorce a plan, rather than part of his arsenal. Or, perhaps, he held on to some hope of eventual reconciliation.

One warm spring day, I agreed to accompany him on the drive out to a suburban hospital, where he served as an attending physician. He hated to make the tedious drive by himself and always tried to recruit one of us kids to go with him. He might also have wanted some time alone with each of us, but he didn't know how to use that time effectively, at least not with me.

He lowered the roof of his large Cadillac convertible, and I sunk into the beige leather seat beside him. Always a fast driver, he flew down the highway. The rush of air swallowed our voices. I was glad we couldn't talk.

"Come the divorce, who are you going to live with?"

I stared out the window.

"Come on, who will you live with?"

I ignored the question until my silence deflated him.

Around this time, I asked my mother if she still loved my father. She responded that her love was like something frozen. I remember wondering what might produce a thaw. I see now that she was speaking about more than their relationship. She, herself, seemed encased in ice. Her impassiveness may be why I underestimated her pain over my father's later relationship with Carol.

A guest at my father's fiftieth birthday party, I sit on carpeted stairs in Carol's finely appointed house. Eighteen and about to complete my freshman year at Penn, I have accepted that I have no influence over my father's choices. I hear laughter and the tinkle of crystal, but I am not inclined to join the festivities. I feel both sad and guilty to be part of a celebration from which my mother has been excluded. My parents live parallel lives and my father the far more appealing one. His world appears expansive, full of productive work and pleasure, while everything about my mother's life is growing smaller.

Shortly after this party, my father rented an apartment in the suburbs. His stated rationale was that he needed to establish residency in the area to enable my youngest brother, Henry, to attend a new school, as he had not thrived in his previous one. But I think the move had more to do with my father's desire for distance from Pine Street and from my mother.

My mother withdrew into misery. It felt as if she were vanishing, alcohol and depression overwhelming her. These twins fed on each other. She once said that depression was like a long dark tunnel from which you could not escape. I thought this the observation of a trained clinician; I didn't understand she was speaking about herself. What she didn't say is that depression covers others in its darkness.

My parents stopped fighting, or, to put it more accurately, my mother stopped. My father continued, at least for a time.

He put his faith in meanness, as if that would be sufficient to engage her. "She's a drunk, worthless, a liar," he'd say, but she seemed not to be paying attention. I never told my parents that this verbal abuse had an insidious effect, worse than the yelling and violence, though if that hadn't stopped, perhaps I would feel differently. I resented my mother's descent into her somber and solitary world. But instead of understanding her behavior—the drinking, despondency, lethargy—as symptoms of severe depression, I believed she had a choice. She could leave her bed and reenter the world, my world. When she didn't, I had only my father's interpretation for the reasons why.

A few years ago, shortly after Carol's death, her daughter told me that her mother had described my father as "the great love of her life." Hearing that, I thought, *I don't care*. I felt affection for her after my father died, because she was bereft, but I never truly warmed to her.

A year or two before my father died, he told Billy that he thought he might have to marry Carol at some point, not so much out of desire but because he thought it was the right thing to do, given her unwavering loyalty.

Did he love her? I suppose he did in his fashion, but not as she did him.

I don't know what my father felt for my mother, other than anger. I never dared ask. Now I see his behavior as rooted in a kind of love, corrupted, but love, nonetheless. He never stopped trying to get her attention.

My father's sudden death fixed my parents' marriage in time as it existed then. How might their relationship have changed over the years they did not have? Would they have returned to each other, rediscovered the happiness so evident in their wedding photo? Probably not. Most likely, they would have remained as they were when last together, in limbo between withdrawal and attraction.

My mother survived my father by thirty-three years. In all those years, whenever she spoke of him, it was with humor and what I now recognize as love. She never sought to turn me against him. I also witnessed some of his worst behaviors, and so might have agreed with her had she chosen to denigrate him. Instead, she let me come to my own conclusions.

In anticipation of her death, my mother said that she wanted my father's ashes scattered with hers, not comingled but released into the ocean at the same time. Her ashes were the consistency of cake flour, my father's coarser with bits of carbon and bone. She had whittled herself down to nothing before she died, while he had been obese—or at least that's how the autopsy described his body—but I never saw him that way.

On a June morning, my brothers, my sister, and I set out into Penobscot Bay off the coast of Maine. White clouds scudded across the pale blue sky. A soft breeze ruffled the indigo water. Sunshine warmed our faces. Our captain settled the boat near a small island, a spot we'd chosen to be able to find it again from the shore. An osprey circled above, close enough to see her white belly and the brown-and-white pattern on her wings, before she veered off to tend her nest. A seal, his black eyes alight with curiosity, floated just off the stern. And dolphins arrived with their perpetual grins. The company would have so pleased my mother. My father too. Poured into the sea, their ashes became moving clouds, as if galaxies were forming. For a few moments, they touched.

The Girl with the Brown Costume

The summer before my mother died, we had one of our last conversations about her past. I remember being surprised at her energy on the phone, her willingness to talk longer than I'd expected. By then, the bad days—hours in which her chronic pain assaulted her—outnumbered the good, though she never complained.

I asked her to tell me about her "great loves," men she had known before she met my father. I am not sure what prompted my question, except that we had never really talked about her romantic history, and I was curious. Also, I like to think that, for once, I chose a subject about which I had no preconceived ideas, leaving my mother freer to reminisce and me to listen.

Margrieta met John Sullivan—the man she thought she would marry—in Vienna shortly after the war ended, most likely at the home of Dr. Boch, the professor of literature who had befriended her. A British officer and member of the Royal Army Medical Corps, he was stationed with the Allied occupation forces.

In a photograph my mother kept of him, he stands with a straight back, his arms relaxed at his sides, a soldier's bearing. He possesses dark eyes and heavy brows, a Roman nose, full lips over a strong chin—a striking face some would find handsome.

John was Irish, from Belfast. Armed with this information and his full name, I searched the internet and found his obituary, published in January 1972 in the *British Medical Journal.* He died suddenly, of causes not disclosed, at age fifty-seven, in Belfast, where he served as senior urologist to the Belfast City Hospital and clinical lecturer at Queen's University. My mother, forty-eight when he died, never learned of his passing.

The photograph is unmistakably the man my mother knew some twenty-five years earlier. He has the same distinctive features, the same confidence I saw in the set of his mouth at thirty-one.

His obituary is full of accolades, offered by a fellow physician, someone who first encountered him during the war: "This keen young officer from Ulster soon became my surgical partner, setting himself with a quiet, kindly skill to anything that needed doing—transfusions and operations, ward rounds with shaded hurricane lamp, feeding the wounded, or writing letters for them." John's affability and attendant charm would have appealed to my young mother.

My mother once told me, "I could fall in love with a lumberjack sexually, but I could never marry him." I didn't remind her that it was unlikely she'd known or would meet a lumberjack, but I understood her point. She had standards in regard to a prospective husband and love alone wasn't sufficient. She sought a mate with a comparable social and educational background, someone with similar aspirations. John came from a prominent family and was cultured and established professionally as an officer and surgeon. He embodied the kind of man Margrieta would consider marrying.

Another photograph captures John and Margrieta on a summer outing with friends—a picnic by a lake. The men wear bathing suits; the women, shorts. John's arm encircles Margrieta's waist, while she leans into him. His gesture is more possessive than protective. On the back of the photograph, years later, my mother inscribed, "Me at my most lovely, with John the Skunk." She had invested her hopes in him, and that misjudgment grated.

John was married, but as his relationship with Margrieta progressed, he insisted that he intended to divorce his wife and marry her. His assurances of love and commitment not only persuaded Margrieta of his sincerity but also convinced Dr. Boch and Margrieta's childhood friend Tamara. Tamara told Margrieta, "The world will spin off its axis before John abandons you."

John made his claims so public, at times even referring to Margrieta as the woman he would marry, that his well-connected family heard of them, and arranged through military channels to have him recalled to London.

The mother I knew would have demonstrated skepticism in regard to John's assurances, but at twenty-two, that woman did not yet exist.

She believed the tales spun by this polished and debonair British officer with whom she had fallen in love. She accepted that his marriage, though perhaps once affectionate and stable, had been shattered by the cataclysm of war. She believed whatever he told her, but especially that she, alone, could ensure his future happiness by marrying him. So confident in his love, she sent some of her belongings with him to London, anticipating she would join him there. Dr. Boch secured a job for her as a nanny to the children of friends in England so that she would have work and a place to live while John extricated himself from his former life.

I picture Margrieta packing. Sunlight streams in from the window yet doesn't warm her spartan bedroom. She notices dust on the headboard and on the small table next to the bed, but housekeeping isn't a concern. She is leaving. She puts her suitcase on the bed and opens the closet, selects two wool skirts, her fitted jacket, a pair of sturdy shoes, the pale blue cashmere sweater John likes her to wear—not too much, but enough for a beginning. "Mrs. Sullivan," she whispers to herself, experimenting with her new name, her new identity. *Will I like England*, she wonders, *and eventually Ireland?* My mother embraced, as only the very young can, the vision of the shared future John had so diligently cultivated.

After John departed for England, Margrieta waited—days then weeks—for him to send word. Each morning, as she awakened without having heard from him, she would tell herself today would be the day her new life would beckon. She would receive a letter or telegram urging her to come to London. Dr. Boch and Tamara tried to remain encouraging, but in private they would have expressed doubt, surprise too, because they'd also believed.

Margrieta didn't want to accept that John had abandoned her, that everything he had promised had been a mirage. She wrote him letters, each one more insistent. His unresponsiveness made her desperate, as if she herself had become something insubstantial. Finally, she sent him a telegram threatening to kill herself if he didn't answer. My mother later assured me that she didn't intend suicide, but she couldn't think of any other way to force John to respond. Regardless of what she suspected, not knowing was worse than anything he might say, because his silence consumed her with both doubt and hope.

John's letter, when it finally arrived, claimed that he would always love her, but his father had reminded him that "he had made his bed and now must lie in it."

Margrieta's hands tremble as she reads his words. *He's a liar . . . he never loved me*, she thinks. She brushes her cheeks with the back of her hand, angry at her own tears, tries to quiet the internal voice taunting her, *You loved him. You wanted the life he offered.* That vision of her future now lies in ruins.

John's obituary reveals something of the life he led: "He was a keen and regular golfer. He had a lovely home and a beautifully kept garden, for both he and his charming wife were keen gardeners. They were also the most delightful and considerate of hosts. A regular worshipper all his life at the Presbyterian church in Bloomfield, his steady Christian faith shown forth in a life of cheerful sympathy for his fellow men."

A life of predictable pleasures, the "bed he had made," and most likely one in which his sleep remained untroubled.

John's obituary describes a future my mother might have lived, had she married him. I cannot envision the mother I knew enjoying that world of gardening and genteel parties, Sunday church services—a world of graceful domesticity—though aspects of it appeal to me, given the contrast with Pine Street. I am drawn to the apparent security and comfort of such an existence, one rooted in a sense of community, a life in which it would be easy to thrive.

To say that my mother held a grudge would be an understatement, though she didn't spend time nurturing her resentment; nevertheless, she never forgave John. When Belfast erupted in violence, my mother admitted to being secretly pleased, but only because she associated the city with him. Long before I learned anything else about their affair, I knew "John the Skunk" as a villain.

My mother believed John had made a fool of her, and that may be what eventually bothered her the most. I don't think she was ever willing to risk that again. She would never, no matter how much she loved a man, allow herself to be that trustful.

My father used to wear orange on St. Patrick's Day. My brother Billy suggested that he did so to irritate our mother by reminding her of John's Protestant Irish roots. Some latent jealousy may also have been at play. Assuming our mother told our father of past loves—and she would have, at least where some were concerned—he would have recognized that he had not been my mother's first choice.

I wonder who my twenty-two-year-old mother would have become had she married John, a man nine years older and far more settled than she. Though that stability may have been part of his appeal, what would have happened to her plans to become a doctor, to immigrate to the United States? I fear she would have molded herself to fit his life, without giving herself the time needed to mature into her own.

My mother's voice softened when she spoke of Viktor Groff, a "wonderful boy," she said.

In 1948, at the age of twenty-one, Viktor fled his native Hungary for Austria to escape the Soviets and the pall Communism had cast over his country. According to my mother, he had been working for the Americans, the Cold War entrenched by then, and they got him out. He left behind his two younger brothers and parents, though they ultimately joined him in the United States following the 1956 Hungarian Revolution.

Margrieta, twenty-five years old in 1948, met Viktor in Salzburg, the city to which she had moved after completing medical school at the University of Vienna. She lived at Glasenbach, a camp for displaced persons on the northeast edge of the city. She had to establish her status as *displaced* from her homeland, rather than a *refugee*, the distinction important. A refugee can return to her country after war's end; Margrieta could not. Her native Latvia had been subsumed into the Soviet Union, leaving her stateless.

Glasenbach stood on a bare expanse of ground above railway yards. Margrieta slept in a small room, one of many in a long wooden building, the space equipped with a metal cot, a single chair, and a table. A portable coal-burning stove occupied one corner and provided some heat when fuel was available. Flimsy walls separated her from neighbors, her privacy one more thing sacrificed.

She might listen to the rumble of trains at night, sometimes a whistle far off, a call in the darkness. Perhaps she comforts herself with the thought that she, too, will be moving on, eventually arriving where she belongs. Glasenbach served as another step in her quest to immigrate to the United States, the only country she believed strong enough to stand up to the Soviet Union.

Margrieta and Viktor both worked for the Lutheran World Federation, an international organization dedicated to assisting refugees and displaced persons. With each successful resettlement, they must have wondered when their turns would come. Aside from the need for medical clearance—only granted to healthy individuals—immigration required a sponsor, someone to offer assurances of housing and a job. Margrieta had both, while Viktor's situation was less encouraging.

It is as if I know Viktor, or at least the part of him that loved my mother. After she died, and I started going through her boxes of keepsakes, the scattered photographs and albums, I discovered his letters. Eight in all, written over a span of thirty years. Aside from a single paragraph in German, he wrote in English—his command of the language progressing from adequacy to mastery.

His missives describe a life at a remove from her, eventually a fulfilling one—a satisfying academic career in comparative literature, "a stable and happy marriage, two handsome sons and a blue-eyed tomboy of a daughter"—but the letters always return to their shared months in Austria.

Viktor's memories of my mother animate a woman I never knew. Marriage and the birth of her children changed her, as did the corrosive effects of unacknowledged trauma. So did the passage of time, as it does for us all.

Viktor's first letter is from Salzburg, February 1950, on the eve of my mother's twenty-seventh birthday. The onionskin paper, a pale canary color, has been folded and refolded. It feels like autumn leaves, about to shred.

My mother had arrived in New York City after a stormy transatlantic crossing some two months earlier. A New York City cabdriver gave her a tour of Manhattan before depositing her at Pennsylvania Station. He wouldn't accept payment, giving her the free ride as a welcome gift to America. She remained a staunch defender of New York cabbies for the rest of her life.

I picture her sitting on the train bound for Philadelphia. Determined to look elegant, she wears a finely made Persian lamb coat with a shawl collar, a belted wool dress with padded shoulders, and polished dress oxfords. Her cardboard suitcase disintegrated during the customs inspection, so her belongings are tied up in a blanket by her side. On her lap she balances a half gallon of strawberry ice cream, napkins, and several plastic spoons. She forces herself to pause between spoonfuls, reminding herself that she wants to appear poised, not ravenous.

She had wanted to make her home in California, but a medical internship at Methodist Episcopal Hospital, a position she had never expected to attain, kept her in Philadelphia. I asked her once about her first impressions of the city and she told me she found it "constipated," which in my mother's parlance meant overly conservative. When I pressed her for something positive, she described Horn and Hardart Automats, where she could get a hard roll and butter for less than a dime, a complete meal for a dollar. She once survived in Vienna for two weeks with nothing more than a bag of jelly beans and cigarettes, so that kind of abundance made an impression.

Viktor, lonely and discouraged about his own future, wishes her happiness and fulfillment in her new country. He likens her to a bird finally set free. I am drawn to that image of my mother with wings because I never knew her unencumbered.

"Our world is so poor and ruined," Viktor writes, "we cannot afford losing the color you mean in it. Preserve it, please." And finally, he reminds her that in his heart and memories she will remain "the girl with the brown costume."

Viktor must be referring to what my mother wore, maybe the dress she had on the first time he saw her. Perhaps he recognized immediately what he would feel for my mother.

Tom remembers what I was wearing the first time he saw me—blue jeans and a blue-and-white-striped oxford shirt with white cuffs. I was ahead of him in line, waiting to schedule time on Wharton's computers. I sat on a table, unaware of his presence. Tom likes to say that he fell in love with me at first sight. I like believing him.

The first time I noticed Tom's clothing, I saw him from a distance crossing the bridge that linked one part of the campus to another. He sported a powder-blue three-piece suit in some material distantly related to wool. I discovered later that the vest, in a stunning example of misguided practicality, reversed to a paisley pattern.

I cannot identify the moment I truly saw the man who became my beautiful, and sometimes elegant, husband, but I was slower then to recognize inner worth, in myself and in him.

Viktor and Margrieta had parted at the Salzburg train station—Margrieta bound for Bremerhaven, Germany, and the ship that would carry her to the United States, while Viktor remained in Austria.

He might have watched until the train disappeared from view, telling himself he would see her again because he couldn't bear to think otherwise. She had been a kind of home for him, their love a sanctuary.

I have a photograph of the two of them from Salzburg, still early in their relationship. A sunny day—it could be early spring or autumn. A lone vine clings to the otherwise bare wall behind them. Though they both wear coats, Margrieta's is open, the soft scarf she wears loose at her throat. In the damp air, without combs to contain it, her hair frames her face in soft ringlets of brownish gold. She holds something in both hands, a dried wildflower. Viktor's thick hair is combed back from his thin face, more soulful than handsome, but in its own way mesmerizing. They both smile in a manner that looks spontaneous, rather than composed for the photographer. Viktor keeps his hands clasped behind his back, perhaps to resist the urge to put his arm around Margrieta. He isn't yet sure of her feelings, only his own.

Margrieta first befriended Viktor, while he fell in love—quickly and deeply. Her affair with John, along with other wounds she hadn't recognized, may have made her guarded in a way Viktor was not. Or, perhaps, it was simply the difference in age and the related disparity in experience. Margrieta had known other lovers. For Viktor, she would be his first.

Their shared displacement intensified the connection between them. They had both been forced from their homelands by Soviet aggression and at the time of their meeting had no hope of ever returning. For Margrieta, at least, the magnitude of the losses she had endured gave her a sense of possibility. She had already been through the worst and survived it, she told herself, so she could meet whatever challenges she faced. She would craft the life she wanted. Her optimism and confidence contributed to "the color" she brought into Viktor's life.

By the time Viktor wrote his next letter in October of 1953, he had immigrated to Florida. My mother had been married for four months by then, and my parents lived in Philadelphia. I would be born a year later.

Viktor wrote that he was still studying toward his degree, but that he had not forgotten her. Working during the day and attending night school, he earned his BA and MA at the University of Miami. Eventually, he completed a doctorate in comparative literature.

"As long as I live, the memory of a lovable, good, and always broke but hopeful young girl will live with me," he told her. He reminded Margrieta of the two of them walking Salzburg's steep streets "under a starlit sky on a warm summer night . . . hungry and a bit drunk with love, youth, and sour white wine." In a brief reference to her current life, he said, "I admire you for the courage to live your life your way." I wonder how my mother described her life to him. He makes no mention of her marriage, but it seems odd she would not have shared the news. Perhaps her marriage had no bearing on the two of them, because their relationship stood apart, born of another place and time.

Close to twenty years passed before Viktor and my mother exchanged letters again, the contact initiated by her in a phone call to him, one she made around her forty-ninth birthday. I can see her seated in front of the walnut secretary desk at the end of the hallway, leaning forward with her elbow on its surface, the rotary-dial phone's handset cradled against her cheek. She rarely spoke for any length of time on the phone, so I would have noticed. In my memory of that moment, I can hear her—not her words but the timbre of her voice. It conveyed an intimate warmth, and I remember thinking this must be someone about whom she cared.

By then my parents' marriage seemed to be disintegrating, the passion that had once infused it exhausted. And at seventeen and in my senior year of high school, I didn't want to consider my parents' lives. I hungered for my own.

In his February 1972 letter, sent in response to her call, Viktor wrote, "Your kind familiar voice struck me like a blow, like a missile hurled from across the gulf of the past . . . which seemed irrevocably lost and yet in a flash it became real again, because you are there." Hearing from her returned him to that Salzburg train station as if it were yesterday, he said, and "not eight thousand yesterdays ago." If he concentrates, he tells her, he sees the world she has created for herself—complicated, filled with memories, lived-in—but somehow still inhabited by the girl he knew. He attributes to both of them a constancy in character and, at least for him, in feeling.

He notes that his wife, who had answered the phone, recognized my mother as the caller instantly, despite knowing very little about her, other than what she had gleaned from some of Viktor's old photographs. They both wondered what had prompted my mother's call.

I think my mother hoped to revive the part of herself that had inspired Viktor's love. She needed to see herself through his eyes to challenge my father's harsh assessment, or her own, the latter being more injurious, because she would have trusted her own judgment over his. Viktor could remind her of who she had been in Austria—a young woman who believed herself capable of anything to which she had committed. She wanted to feel fearless again. But perhaps what she wanted most of all was to feel loved.

For the next two months, Viktor and my mother maintained contact through letters and by phone. Viktor's March letter is written in response to a letter from my mother. She proposed visiting him and wondered if his wife would like her. I find myself considering the same question. I suspect Elizabeth's response would not have depended on her opinion of my mother but on her assessment of the state of her own marriage. Viktor writes that he would be happy to see her but wants her to wait. He is not ready to share her, or the part of his life defined by their relationship. Their history is "salient" to his identity, and he wishes to keep it separate from his wife and children, with whom he has shared almost everything else.

Viktor and my mother treated their common history the same way, as something to safeguard, a past whose power would be diminished if subjected to the scrutiny of others. Viktor also feared that his children would find meeting my mother disorienting. They consider their own births, he explained, "the cosmic event which began all that is significant." His children would be shocked to discover their father's earlier life.

The same might be said of me. Because of my mother's influence on me, I sometimes exaggerate my own on her. I have no past in which she is not present, at least in some way. In contrast, she lived a life before mine, lives really, about which I know only what she chose to reveal.

Viktor returned photographs to my mother with his March letter, as requested, including the one she had given him in parting, her words scrawled over her image, "I love you and always will. Never forget it." Below that he had added, "Remember? I do . . ." The power of their love affair lay there, in memory, where it could be preserved against the influence of time, a love that need never be tested.

My mother may have asked for the old photographs because she wanted further evidence of a past she treasured. Viktor and my mother's relationship had sustained them within a world devastated by war, ruination they hoped their children would never know. The images of my mother from Austria also recalled the years during which she believed she had been most lovely. And most hopeful.

In April of 1972, Viktor wrote to my mother again, apparently in response to another conversation by phone. He brings her up to date on an opportunity for a new job at a small college in the north of Florida. Though an academic demotion, he hopes to get the position, because it would afford him and his family everything he wants in a hometown—a rural setting with good hunting and fishing nearby, pristine white beaches on an unspoiled bay. I think how lovely it might be to privilege place over professional ambition. That ordering of priorities would never have occurred to my parents, and, perhaps as a result, it didn't occur to me. But I have come to appreciate the influence of place, the ways in which a particular geography, both domestic space and the external landscape, might prove nurturing.

The second paragraph of Viktor's letter is in German, a language my mother and he shared, though they rarely used it when together, relying instead on English. He chose to write in German to reveal some of what he had wanted to tell her when they last spoke, but could not because his younger son was always nearby. He wonders why he didn't think of speaking to her in German then.

He writes that despite all that has happened to them over the course of their lives, she is still "the beloved." He remains forever grateful for her love, he assures her, of which he was not worthy. He hopes that they will meet again, telling her that regardless of when and where that may be, for them, it will always be spring in the places they knew together—an inn beside a turquoise lake, under the spruce trees high above Salzburg. "We are partners in secrets I could never share with anyone else. I only have to close my eyes, and I see you again—in moods of reflection and passion." He thanks her for coming back into his life.

The letter's last paragraph returns to a chattier tone, in which Viktor describes his family's garden and expresses his hope that spring, the "loveliest season," is underway in Philadelphia. He notes that he has enclosed a photograph of "the whole crew," as he'd promised last time.

I do not have the sense that Viktor's enduring love for my mother compromised his feelings for or devotion to his wife and children. I believe the same of my mother. She didn't reach out to Viktor in hopes she might rekindle an old romance. Though the character of her marriage differed significantly from what I understand of Viktor's, she remained loyal to my father.

A year later, in March 1973, Viktor wrote to my mother again. It was the previous summer, he reminds her, when he last heard from her. He takes responsibility for the lapse in communication but explains that his "times have been somewhat distressing and bewildering." In August, after months of terrible pain, his mother died of cancer. On that same day, the last truckload of the family's belongings departed the Florida home Viktor and his family had shared since the 1950s. In light of these endings, the entire month seemed like a "sad nightmare." He thinks it likely my mother tasted a similar despair when the Soviets took over Latvia, and perhaps again when they were the first to occupy Vienna.

He writes that he and his family have settled into their new home in northern Florida and he is easing into small-town living. His new teaching job is not particularly challenging, and that "is just as well."

Viktor's penultimate letter dates from June of 1980 and is in response to a phone call from my mother after a gap of eight years. At the University of Illinois doing research, Viktor writes, "It is always a joy to know that you are well and full of plans, with the future opening up new vistas." The plans to which he refers involve my mother's anticipated move to Texas.

Viktor could not have known the reasons for her silence, but I remember those years as a time marked by a steady erosion of her mental health. Her world shrunk to the confines of our house, then her bedroom, and, finally, her bed.

My father's sudden death a year earlier served as the catalyst for her move, though I do not think my mother would have managed it without a family friend. Patricia knew Texas from having worked in Dallas for a time and wanted to return to the state. She convinced my mother that the move made sense for her as well, and then helped in its realization. My mother was easily persuaded. I think she wanted to escape Pine Street, perhaps realizing that remaining there in isolation with her memories would be her undoing.

My mother lived in Texas for close to thirty years, initially in McAllen and then in Fredericksburg, between Austin and San Antonio, in a part of the country the rest of us—my brothers, my sister, and I—never came to know. She claimed to love Texas, in part, because she believed Texans possessed independent spirits. "I like the wide open spaces," she said, even though she didn't explore them. She appreciated the possibility of adventure.

Viktor sent his last letter a month later, in July, while still working at the University of Illinois. The narrow bed on which he slept in graduate housing made him remember the rich softness of a bed they once shared at a hotel by Lake Fuschl, near Salzburg, the jeweled lake surrounded by forested mountains, a place he associated with my mother. He reminds her of their sexual relationship and her role as a "lovely teacher" and his as "an eager pupil." When he was young, he tells her, he didn't appreciate lovemaking as the profound experience it is: "The intimacy transcends our bodies; in it we defeat mortality and loneliness." He closes his letter, "My memories bring you back with pine needles in your hair, your glorious beauty smiling down on me . . . Remember?"

Viktor lived with his family in Florida for another twenty-eight years, dying four years before my mother. He and my mother were not in touch again, but I do not believe either of them would have considered that an ending.

Until I read Viktor's letters, I hadn't realized that his relationship with my mother had continued beyond Salzburg, albeit at a distance. In one of them he wrote that every fortunate man has a love experience that doesn't end but "lingers in the background, casting a bit of rosy glow on the drab stuff of life." Without anyone noticing, a part of my mother, the girl dressed in brown, lived in that afterglow.

The Third Thing

My mother's old suitcase calls to me from a shelf in my office, like a book that insists on my reading.

The case's scraped edges reveal brownish tan leather under the navy blue, the surface so worn that if it brushes against my clothes, it leaves brown dust. Rows of careful stitches confirm once fine workmanship. Metal clasps close the case, though the key to lock them is lost.

The interior, lined in silky blue fabric, smells of old paper and leather, forgotten time. The suitcase holds an eclectic collection, an inventory without any organizing principle, other than my mother's desire to safeguard the contents. Some documents provide official certification—of my parents' marriage, my mother's naturalization as an American citizen, my father's death. I find his obituary, the edges frayed, the newsprint smudged.

There are copies of tributes offered by my father's friends and colleagues at numerous memorial services, typed and then signed by the physicians who composed them, their degrees and affiliations longer than their names.

My mother was fifty-six when my father died. She lived without him for more than three decades, alone except for the stories she told.

I uncover a newspaper clipping from *The Valdosta Times* announcing my parents' June 1953 marriage, the paper soft and yellowed. A fawn-colored card from some long-gone insurance company protects the clipping. On the outside of the card is written, "Good news about <u>you</u>!" with an ink drawing of a grinning man in a loose three-piece suit holding a paper aloft. Inside the card is the printed message, "Congratulations, thought you might like to have the clipping." The card looks like an artifact recovered from a civilization now extinct.

There's an out-of-date passport, a recipe for rum cake, and *New Yorker* cartoons featuring dogs.

According to my mother, my first phrase was "See dog," as I pointed to a tiny dog in the corner of a *New Yorker* cartoon. The fact that I focused on something at the periphery, rather than the central image of a crowd of people, struck my mother, as did evidence of my early attachment to dogs, something the two of us shared. Maybe as a result of being so small myself, I gravitated toward the miniature. Or, perhaps, I was drawn to what lay outside the frame because I somehow recognized that I would dwell there.

I find photographs of myself as a newborn, black-and-white images on heavy stock paper, one of them in a cardboard frame from Lorraine Studio, Ardmore, Pennsylvania. I am reminded of Rodin's *The Thinker*, if he were presented as an infant and reclining rather than sitting. More images exist of me in infancy than of my sister and brothers, perhaps because I was my parents' first, born before the crowding of time.

"I want to tell you how you were conceived," my mother announced at the start of one of our interviews. In an earlier conversation I had asked her to tell me anything she thought I should know, but I hadn't expected her to return to my birth.

It's a November morning and I sit at my desk in a comfortable chair. A large holly fills the window, its green leaves and delicate berries shiny in the damp air. The statuesque holly gets pride of place in a way it doesn't in the midst of summer's abundance. Scarcity can engender its own kind of beauty, because we recognize with deeper clarity what remains.

Several states away, my mother relaxes in her recliner by the sliding glass door to her terrace, her cordless phone in her hand. The weather in Concord warmer than in Pittsburgh that day, the sky a vivid blue. Sunlight shines on my mother's shoulders. Outside, autumn's radiance, in spots of deep orange and yellow, lingers. Or, perhaps, I only wish the weather to be so, as if by prolonging this season of endings I might give us more time.

Tom and I will spend Thanksgiving with my mother in Massachusetts. It wouldn't have occurred to me to wait and conduct the interview in person. My choice made sense in some ways—the holiday would be crowded with other activities—but talking by phone was easier and more familiar. I'd grown accustomed to our circumscribed relationship in the thirty years we'd lived in different parts of the country. The physical distance, I realize now, protected me from too much hope. I could tell myself that our periodic phone calls sustained our relationship in a kind of holding pattern. Closeness remained something in the future, a destination I'd eventually reach.

"When I married Daddy, we decided that we would not have children until he finished his residency, but I was worried that I wouldn't be able to conceive," my mother explained. She feared that her third abortion in Vienna and the subsequent infection had scarred her uterus.

"Even though the two of you had already conceived a child?" I asked, reminding her of their pregnancy before they married. "Pardon?" she responded, but I persisted for a few more beats.

I tended to insist on accuracy, an adherence to verifiable facts and, absent those, consistency with whatever she had conveyed earlier. I realize now that the subject of my mother's anecdote—in this case, my conception and birth—isn't as important as what motivated her account. She wanted me to understand her desire.

"I was delighted that I got pregnant, even though it wasn't planned. And then I worried that I was too old." At thirty-one, according to medical opinion at the time, my mother was old to be having her first child. "But you were born perfectly healthy, and I was very happy."

Since my father had wanted to delay children, and because my parents had terminated that earlier pregnancy, I asked about my father's reaction.

"Well, he accepted it and he was glad for the baby in the end."

I wanted to know if he had suggested they end the pregnancy. "Oh, no. God forbid, no," she said. "He did not. No, he did not."

As was more typical then, my mother's obstetrician induced labor and delivered me using forceps. "You were a perfectly wonderful baby. There was no distortion of your skull, which can happen with a normal delivery," she said. "You were absolutely beautiful. The nurses commented on your beauty. You opened your eyes right after delivery practically. Oh, God, you were a beautiful baby." I hear the pride in my mother's voice, admiration too, as she remembers our beginning. I scan the images of me as a newborn and find what my mother saw. Dark almond-shaped eyes with feathered brows light up my tiny face. I *was* beautiful.

I am surprised to uncover another photograph of me, older, also from a photographer's studio. Few photographs were taken of us as children, and those that existed were not displayed. If you wandered through our house, you would not find framed images on tables or shelves, art on the walls, or plants except one struggling potted palm. The house offered no clues about what its inhabitants valued.

I am about five and wear a gingham dress with puffy short sleeves. My hair is in a pixie style, its bright sheen emphasizing my deep brown eyes. I'd cut my hair on my own not long before, I think, so the short style would have been an accommodation to those results.

Someone in the house, my grandmother Lee or my mother, had been trimming her hair, and it gave me the idea to do the same. I took my surprisingly sharp toy scissors and set to work. I didn't use a mirror, just snipped away. I liked the way the blades felt close to my scalp, so I kept opening and closing them in the same spot. When I finally looked in the mirror and saw the rough patchwork my hair had become, my mouth formed an *O* of astonishment. I feared I'd done something terrible.

I trudged downstairs to the kitchen, where my mother was cooking. I had faith she could somehow restore my hair, or, if a miracle of that magnitude were not possible, she'd think of something else. "Mommy," I said. She turned from the stove, raised her free hand to her mouth, and burst into laughter. The moment marked the first time I realized someone was laughing at me. Though my mother's response didn't feel mean, I disliked it all the same. I started to cry.

By the time I reached adolescence, my hair had taken on an exaggerated importance in my family; my mother, in particular, demonstrated a proprietary interest.

When I was eleven or so and Billy about eight, an argument with him escalated into physical violence. Taller and heavier, I still had a slight advantage, though I was rapidly losing it. When he reached to yank my hair, my mother shouted, "No, not the hair!" We both paused, startled by her interference, and then continued pummeling each other. I wonder now why she didn't stop the fight, but only limited its scope.

❧ ❧ ❧

I find still more photographs, including one of me in my first formal gown, a bridesmaid dress in lavender chiffon. Within the photo's cardboard frame, my mother added loose photos, one of Tom, and more baby pictures of me. I suppose she wanted the protection the cardboard offered, but I look at the images and think of her crafting a story: A beautiful baby girl grows into a pretty young woman, who goes on to marry a handsome prince. A pleasing tale, and because I did marry a wonderful man, the narrative is true in a simplistic sense, but I've found that *happily ever after* misses the point. Marriage isn't an ending. Marriage is a beginning.

What made my mother retain these photographs? She must not have looked at them often—they were tucked away in an old suitcase—but she kept them safe for decades. They reveal that I had her attention when I hadn't believed that to be true.

I would have been twenty-two in the photograph and just graduated from the University of Pennsylvania. My skin glows a peachy brown, tanned by hours spent sunbathing on the tar roof of our house. I smile toward the camera, my full mouth closed. Silver drop earrings catch the light. I wear my long hair in a bun, a strong middle part visible, something I share with my mother.

As a young woman, I had beautiful hair, chestnut with auburn highlights. My mother told me she had conjured me as a brunette while I waited in her womb. "Blondes always look washed out without makeup," she used to say. She wore her own blonde hair swept up in a French twist and advised me to adopt a similar style. "I don't like it when you wear your hair down," she'd tell me. I sometimes wondered what the point was of having long hair if I always confined it, though I recognized the elegance of the styles she recommended. I realize now that aesthetic preferences may not have been her only motivation. It seems to me that she was also counseling me to hold something in reserve, to not *let my hair down* in a deeper sense of keeping my distance. She was warning me against emotional vulnerability. Or, perhaps, I absorbed that message from the way she behaved.

Her influence led me to keep my hair long for years beyond the time when its quality justified that choice.

Finally, at age fifty, I decided to cut my hair short, aware that it had thinned and lost some of its luster, and hopeful that a dramatic change would improve its condition. I didn't consult my mother beforehand, afraid she would talk me out of it. I did talk to Tom, ceaselessly he might say, until he finally spoke to his hairstylist on my behalf.

"Dani can see you now," he told me over the phone from the salon, where he'd just had his own hair cut. Fifteen minutes later I walked into the brightly lit space, the walls covered in mirrors, swivel chairs in front of the glass. I arrived nervous but also determined to change at least this one thing about myself. Dani and I looked through books of various hairstyles. Tom offered opinions when asked, without trying to force me to come to a decision. Though none of the images captured exactly what I wanted, my conversation with Dani increased my confidence in her, and in myself. I made an appointment for the following Saturday.

A week later, I sat in the salon chair, my hair a carpet of brown grass around me. I felt lighter, freer, as though something heavy I'd been carrying had been set aside. *How ridiculous*, I thought, *to have waited so long in doubt of my own judgment*.

Later, my mother asked what my hair looked like, and I told her, "Imagine a crown of dark flowers."

Physical attractiveness mattered to my mother. She recognized beauty's power and wished to wield it to her advantage. She certainly talked about how people looked. In particular, she commented on women's figures—men too, but she reserved her more detailed assessments for women—directing a particular harshness toward women who were overweight, unless she knew them personally. In those instances, she'd replace her criticism with the expressed hope that they would diet.

During my last visit to Texas, not long before my mother moved to Massachusetts, she criticized someone's girth, though I don't remember whose. It could have been an actor on television, as the TV was on.

"Why do you always have to comment when someone is fat? It's the first thing you say about them."

Silence. My mother stares at the TV, her jaw set.

"Really, Mom. Why?"

"Because I suffered very much from being fat as a child." Her beautiful mother would have ridiculed her, and if she didn't, the invariable comparisons between them would have hurt.

"So, what . . . now you want to make everyone else suffer? If someone is fat, believe me, they know it. You don't have to tell them."

"I want to help them reduce."

"Did being told you were fat help you? It's as though you define people that way. How would you have described Dad? He was fat. Is that the first thing you would have said? He was also an accomplished surgeon, a brilliant man."

My mother doesn't respond, and I let the matter drop, though I don't accept her explanation that a desire to be of assistance motivates her criticism. I think her own painful memories of humiliation drive her to focus on this vulnerability.

I always dieted in advance of visits, as the prospect of seeing my mother increased my resolve to shed however much weight stood between me and my vision of slimness. I sought thinner thighs, narrower hips, a flat stomach. When I'd succeeded in denying my hunger for long enough that my appetite disappeared, I knew I was losing weight.

I wanted my mother to find me beautiful, her opinion on the subject more important than my own. Looking good felt like a shield, one that gave me a sense of confidence and control.

It's May 2009 and I stand in my mother's apartment in Massachusetts for the first time since her move from Texas three months earlier. "Stand up straight," she used to insist. "You don't want to get a dowager's hump." That warning—that I would develop a permanent curve in the upper part of my back if I didn't hold my head up with shoulders erect—seemed idle commentary when I was young, just another one of my mother's admonitions about appearance.

I lift my spine and relax my shoulders, hold what I believe is a dancer's stance. *Let her get a good look at me*, I think. I wait to sit down on my mother's sofa, wanting first to present myself to advantage.

I've put on makeup—dark liner to emphasize my eyes—and run gel through my short hair to accentuate the curl. I wear slim jeans, a fitted jacket by an edgy Japanese designer, sleek boots. The jeans hug my hips in a way that feels like success.

On this early May day the sun shines, ribbons of light flashing through the shades on the door to my mother's terrace. Trees are leafing in that tender green, a color no sooner recognized than it begins to darken. The air outside so fresh that within the apartment it feels stagnant and suddenly too warm. My mother finally within reach, and I am not ready.

She sits in her recliner, her wheeled walker nearby, but I still believe the walker is optional. She smiles at me, her eyes alight. "Do you know what it feels like to love someone so much it hurts?"

I tense, remain silent. And I think, *Yes, that's how it is between us, our efforts to love each other painful.* My anger surprises me.

I look back on that interval with regret, because I see the opportunity missed. Why couldn't I respond to my mother's overtures? I wouldn't even allow myself to believe her, not about the pain—I got that part—but about her love. I suppose what I wanted to say was I know exactly what it means to love someone so much it hurts, and it's not about the fear of losing them. It's a fear that love will never be enough.

I keep returning to the suitcase, as if in conversation with my mother. Finding myself so present within both surprises and pains me. She never told me what these mementos meant to her, rarely said anything that would have led me to expect to discover myself among them. It was as if these photographs and papers represented stand-ins for us, placeholders for an unrealized intimacy.

I unearth newspaper clippings my mother saved, folded accordion style, so that I have to smooth them flat in order to read them. When Tom and I lived in Pittsburgh, we were sometimes photographed at charity events, our involvement expected as part of Tom's corporate responsibilities. One story profiled us as honorary co-chairs for a gala benefiting the Pittsburgh Film Office. The reporter called us a "power couple," a description that would have pleased my mother.

She was especially proud of Tom, whose professional achievements and stature she celebrated. I hadn't known he'd kept her informed on this score, and that she'd carefully tucked the evidence away. I find articles from decades ago. One piece from *American Banker*, "40 Under 40," identifies Tom as a young professional to watch. Another announces Tom's first important promotion within the financial services company for which he worked, marking the beginning of his ascent into executive management. He ended up as a vice chairman, reporting to the

CEO of that same financial services company, by then one of the largest in the United States.

I, too, am proud of Tom's professional achievements, substantial by any objective measure. But I've known others with similar accomplishments. My husband's personal attributes make him noteworthy, far more than his successful career. He is a man of deep integrity and intelligence, qualities my mother also valued. Sometimes I say that a great deal was made up to me when I married Tom, even though I recognize that life doesn't work that way. Childhood unhappiness doesn't entitle you to future joy. Sometimes a painful history only begets more sorrow.

There's a more recent photograph of Tom at work, taken during some kind of presentation to employees. The image captures him in profile, the crisp collar of his white shirt visible, a flash of red from his tie. He's grinning at someone, an expression on his face I've seen so many times, starting with photographs of him as a small boy. Behind him a screen projects "Grow PNC," a reference to his employer. Tom inscribed the photograph, "Mom, I thought you might want to see me 'in action' at work. Love, Tom."

She would have first noticed his handsome appearance. "Tom gets better looking with age," she liked to tell me. She believed herself closer to him than was his own mother, and I never corrected her. She certainly expressed her affection for him with less restraint. "My Tommy," she would say, her hands on his shoulders as she leaned in for a kiss.

My mother's love for Tom enhanced her relationship with me. I valued her recognition of his fineness; it was a judgment on which we agreed. But there was more to it. My mother and I needed someone or something between us, some third thing to allow us to connect.

⚜ ⚜ ⚜

It's a few days before Christmas, and my mother is visiting Tom and me in Pittsburgh for what will turn out to be the last time. A balsam fir, a tree with a heady pine scent, stands in a corner of our family room in front of the large window overlooking the backyard. Visible outside, a palette of taupe and brown and then the deep green of hemlocks at the base of the fenced-in yard, the barrier installed to safeguard our dogs, Gilbert and Annie. In a stiff breeze, the hemlocks' branches remind me of the fluttering hands of women unaccustomed to stillness. The air outside damp, but not really cold, except for the way the moisture in the air chills.

The sky is turning to violet, lingering between day's end and night's beginning. The black branches of the oak tree, the tallest near our house, draw my gaze, the oak's skeleton visible now. The winter landscape surrounds my mother and me—with its more subtle hues, the trees without leaves beautiful in their austerity, the evergreens lush in a geography pared down to the essential. I want to think about aging that way, as a process of refinement. In the end, what endures is what's truest about each of us.

My mother and I sit on the blue leather couch, Gilbert and Annie between us. Right now, it's enough to be together watching the end of day. I stop yearning for this moment to be something more. I rest my hand on one of my dogs, while my mother strokes the other terrier. I watch her palm as it slides over the dog's flank, a comfort to them both. Gilbert's broken coat rougher than Annie's smooth, so that I know them by touch in the dark. Their coats smell of moss and dry leaves.

The dogs' gentle snoring is like the sound of rain. The television is on, but my mother and I talk during the show, so that the broadcast becomes white noise. Occasionally, one of us pays attention, but not for long.

I no longer remember what we talked about; it doesn't matter. Gilbert's and Annie's presence mediated between us, creating a feeling of ease.

My mother used to tell me that sometimes she feared the gods would punish her for her fierce maternal pride. I searched for the story that might have inspired her comment and found the myth of Niobe, Queen of Thebes. Niobe insulted the goddess Leto by boasting of her numerous progeny—seven sons and seven daughters—while the goddess had only two, Apollo and Artemis. She urged the people of Thebes to worship her instead of Leto.

The Greek gods always punished human hubris. To avenge their mother, Apollo, the archer god, and Artemis, the divine huntress, struck down all of Niobe's children. Niobe, seeing them die, collapsed in grief next to their bodies, her tears flowing without end. Zeus took pity on her and transformed her into stone, forever wet with tears.

The death of Niobe's children would have been what spoke to my mother, as the punishment she feared. That's not what resonates with me, perhaps because I do not have children. I think about the loss of Niobe herself, the mortal woman so stupefied by anguish that she became stone. My mother shared some of Niobe's fate. The traumas she endured before my birth calcified parts of her. A grief she didn't recognize for losses she never acknowledged, at least not in ways I understood, walled off parts of her.

In my mother's suitcase I find my bound MFA thesis, paper clips on some pages to mark passages to which she wanted to return. She transcribed sections of the introduction and put the pages in a separate blue folder. I picture her holding a pen in her arthritic hand; it must have been painful to write, but her graceful handwriting, a combination of print and cursive, flows across the yellow legal pages. The content she chose less important to me than her effort. Writing became another third thing between us, allowing us to communicate in a way we could not in person. Taking my words in may have been her way to take me in. She parsed my language in the way I now parse her.

I also uncover one of my essays, "Pine Street," the title a reference to our family home. I wrote this version in an MFA workshop, some six years before my mother's death. She always asked to read my writing, even work that never went beyond early drafts, but this is the only essay she saved, perhaps because we are its central characters.

Initially, I resisted sharing the draft essay with her, because I feared she would find my observations upsetting. The piece represented my first attempt to explore my mother's struggles with depression and alcohol, illnesses I correctly associated with PTSD, but without an adequate understanding of the disorder.

After she read the essay for the first time, she called me. "I'm sorry," she said. I wish I could remember the details of the phone call, because, even then, I recognized its importance. My mother's voice trembled when she spoke, and I wondered if she might start to cry. I said something like, "Oh, Mom, it's all right. Don't worry," trying to move us past her words. Strange to get the apology I thought I wanted—for the home I yearned for but did not have—and then not know how to respond.

On a shelf in my closet, I keep a large blue box. My own third thing. Within, I find birthday cards from years ago, some with messages my mother added to reinforce the ones created by the greeting card company. I think of her browsing the card section of a drugstore or grocery, surprised by her patience. She searches until she finds the card that might speak for her.

In a Christmas card from 1995, a year before Tom and I moved to Pittsburgh, my mother apologizes that her gift could not be wrapped and hangs, instead, in the guestroom closet. She and Tom had gone shopping for clothes for me, and the lovely black dress would not have benefited from being folded into a box, even though they both tried. She remembered how much I liked packages when I was a child. Undoing the ribbons and carefully removing the colorful tissue paper prolonged the pleasure of anticipation. The extra effort required to wrap the gift made it more substantial.

My mother used to tell me how lucky I was in Tom's ability to choose flattering clothes for me. "Do you have any idea how unusual that is?" she'd say. "A man might admire a pretty dress and then buy it for his wife. And the dress might be pretty, but it looked good on a tall slender blonde, and his wife is a curvaceous petite brunette. Tom sees what will work for you."

I reopen a letter from November 1996. My mother sent it on the eve of her flight north to spend Thanksgiving with Billy and Christmas with Tom and me in our new home in Pittsburgh. She provides all the details she can think of to help us navigate her death "in case the plane crashes." Whenever she flew, she feared disaster.

She wants Tom and me, as co-executors of her will, to know that all outstanding bills have been paid. Anything new will be from charges related to her trip and made to one of her three credit cards—each one listed with identifying numbers. We should remember to cancel the cards. She includes a blank check, so we will have her banking details, and reminds us that she has flight insurance through American Express. If she perishes on the plane, we should collect the payment.

After she died, Billy commented that she had been proud of her organized recordkeeping and her disciplined approach to her finances. During the worst of the Pine Street years,

I had no confidence that she could manage the day-to-day tasks of living, and while that may have been true then, she had changed.

My mother might have remained in Texas until her death had my siblings and I not persuaded her to move north to be closer to one of us, in this case, to Concord near Billy and his family. In the end, she offered only token resistance, recognizing that at eighty-six, she needed help to continue to live independently.

Tom and I handled the business related to her relocation—selling her house, financing the purchase of the apartment in Massachusetts—but I didn't go to Texas to help her move. That task fell to Billy and Henry. I told them I didn't have the emotional reserves needed. I would not have found the patience or kindness required. I helped my mother in the ways I could to preserve my own image of myself as a dutiful daughter, not because I found any joy in doing so. My grievances, though I would have been loath to admit it, were dormant but still alive.

While my mother remained in another part of the country and we saw each other infrequently, I could keep her petrified, as if she had been set in amber. I told myself that we loved each other but did so without intimacy. That while my mother might be ready to do anything she could for me, I would never put her to the test. And finally, I persuaded myself that I had arrived at peace with our relationship, because I no longer had any expectations for it. What nonsense. Loving someone means you have expectations.

Another keepsake I cherish, even though I rarely wear them anymore, are gold earrings cast in the shape of leaves. It's not so much the jewelry that retains a hold on me. It is, rather, the image of my mother waiting.

My mother had come north on one of her semiannual visits. She had traveled by train to Philadelphia from New York, where she had spent a week with her friend Daniel and his family. While Tom parked the car, I hurried into 30th Street Station, worried she had already arrived. I saw her seated on a long wooden bench on one side of the station's cavernous waiting area, though she remained unaware of my approach. She looked untroubled, and because I knew she expected me, I guessed that I occupied her thoughts. As I walked toward her, I watched her fiddling with a small cardboard box she cradled in her palm. She kept opening and closing the box, examining the contents. Then she drew out one of the earrings and held it to the light, as if to assure herself, once more, that she had made a good choice. I knew she intended the jewelry for me, an unexpected gift. She looked up at me and smiled.

Homecoming

On the Thursday before my mother's celebration of life party, the tent went up. As soon as that happened, I wanted to call my mother. But then I remembered that the tent was going up because I could no longer call her. And yet she had been present during so much of the planning, as I made choices with her in mind—from the sleek black dress I wore with textured stockings and high heels, to the menu created around roasted pork, to the eulogy I composed and delivered as the first speaker of the afternoon.

On Saturday at 4 p.m., I stood at the podium in one corner of the tent. Our guests sat at round tables covered in white linens, at their centers small vases of flowers and lanterns we would light as the afternoon progressed into evening. I scanned the audience, focusing on the smiles of friends gathered in my mother's honor, many of whom I had not seen in decades. I saw encouragement and an eagerness to hear whatever I had to tell them about the mother I knew and tried to know. And I also saw love. For my mother. For my sister and brothers. And on that day, for me.

⚜ ⚜ ⚜

I had assumed Billy and his wife would host the celebration, as they entertain with graciousness and ease. But a month after our mother's death, Billy asked me to take on that role. Many of the anticipated guests lived in Philadelphia or its environs, and Tom's and my spacious house and surrounding land could accommodate a large gathering. Agreeing to organize a bigger party than I had ever undertaken, and in a home for which extensive renovations were still underway, made me anxious, though that's not why I resisted. A part of me, the part that still lived at Pine Street, wanted to say no.

Yet, I recognized I was being presented with an opportunity—to make amends for not being with my mother when she died, to assert myself as her firstborn, and to strengthen my relationship with my brothers and sister by contributing what they could not. With our mother's death, our family no longer had a matriarch, though I am not sure she saw herself that way. Nevertheless, she acted as the gravitational center around whom the rest of us revolved. Assuming the role of host, even if only for a single event, placed me in unfamiliar territory—at the heart of my family.

We identified a Saturday at the end of September, but in June when we gathered in Maine to scatter our parents' ashes, I moved the party to the end of October to give me more time to settle into our new home. I could not have known that I'd chosen the Saturday when Hurricane Sandy would batter the East Coast. We missed her full force by just over twenty-four hours. I read once that in some Native American cultures, people believe that the release of a great spirit generates extreme weather, as if the universe must respond with equal vibrancy. My mother would have liked the idea, especially since the hurricane did not interrupt, but followed, the celebration of her life.

My brothers, my sister, and I agreed to finance the party with proceeds from our mother's modest estate, before its final distribution to each of us. A few years before our father died, he had established a marital and residual trust: the first of which was to support our mother during her lifetime, and the second to provide supplemental income if needed, or otherwise to be preserved for us, his children. My mother lived frugally during her years in Texas, not unlike her mother had in the years after she immigrated to the United States, and perhaps with similar motivation. I think my mother wanted to ensure that she never had to rely on any of her children for financial support. She would have viewed such dependence as a burden.

I sent invitations to more than one hundred people, including my siblings' extended families. With the exception of Tom's sister Barbara and her husband, we did not invite anyone from Tom's large family—he is the second of seven children—as none of them knew my mother, brothers, or sister. Tom and I brought our two families together for our wedding and did not try to do so again. The two groups seemed so different in interests and perspectives that I believed the best I could hope for between them would be cordiality. I never tested that assumption.

In the weeks leading up to the party, I vacillated between confidence in my ability to manage the elaborate event and what I can only describe as dread.

Most of those invited had shared in the life of Pine Street, sometimes as residents. I realized that the party would be both a celebration of my mother's life and also a kind of reunion. I would be returning to the realm of my childhood and adolescence, a domain in which I had not thrived. My anxiety didn't have anything to do with specific individuals but with what they represented. I feared an invading force that would not respect Tom's and my immaculate and carefully ordered house. I feared destruction. I feared, in this home I had created, feeling like an outsider.

⚜ ⚜ ⚜

My mother never saw the house in which she would be remembered, though when we acquired the property in September 2011, I thought she might. I wanted her approval and confirmation that we had made a good choice. She had visited all of our other homes, first in Philadelphia and then in Pittsburgh, her presence in each a necessary rite of passage.

She worried about our move, reminding me that I had been unhappy in Philadelphia. To reassure her, I told her that I needed to return to the scene of the crime. I referred to *the scene of the crime* flippantly, and it made her smile. I did not want to explain that the source of my unhappiness did not reside in Philadelphia but within our family home.

The past retains its hold, even when we believe we have left it behind. And what we reject can have a greater influence on us than what we embrace. The places I inhabited with Tom, and cultivated as homes to the extent I could, existed in opposition to my family home. I remained tied to Pine Street even as I sought its remaking.

I saw our Paoli property for the first time on a day of unclouded blue sky and warm air that felt like a caress. Mature hedges of burning bush, foliage that turns scarlet in autumn, lined both sides of the driveway, guiding us to the not-yet-visible house. Rather than confusion, the approach encouraged anticipation. A walkway from the driveway led us through the courtyard of brick and stone to the house's entrance. Three statuesque zelkova trees provided shade. Their many soaring branches reminded me of enormous bouquets. A Japanese maple grew to the right of the front door. Sunlight on its red leaves cast a rosy glow on the house's facade.

The exterior environment enchanted me to such a degree that only the most glaring flaws within the house would have caught my attention. But after the previous owner had emptied the place of furniture and art, the grand piano that overwhelmed the living room, I realized that I did not like the interiors. The invitation conveyed by the way we entered the property and the graceful manner in which the house rested within, rather than dominating, the surrounding terrain led me to expect that charm to continue within the house. It didn't, though it took me a few months to understand why.

Renovations undertaken by the former owners lacked a coherent aesthetic. Too many unnecessary doors, harsh track lighting, inexplicable architectural flourishes, floors of different heights, so that we risked tripping when going from one room to the next—all of this accumulated to create a feeling of dissonance. Though this house did not resemble Pine Street in any obvious way, the interiors felt similar in that they existed as disconnected spaces.

At the same time, the Paoli house spoke to me. I wanted to discover and listen to the genius of that house and property. I sensed doing so would teach me something. Or perhaps, it would free me, and that would be sufficient.

In *The Architecture of Happiness*, Alain de Botton suggests that the architectural impulse responds to a longing to declare ourselves to the world through a register other than words, through the language of objects, colors, and bricks. There is a reciprocity between each of us and the places we inhabit. We modify these environments over time, if only by our presence. And we, in turn, are changed. In Paoli, I wanted to create a refuge of peace and beauty. I wanted to achieve there what I had not experienced at Pine Street: the feeling of being home.

Home is both a tangible reality and an abstraction. It encompasses the structures we inhabit and the physical geography of a specific place, as well as the intimate landscape of the heart and spirit. It is a feeling I carry within, but also something I continue to nurture over time. Home is protected intimacy.

When Tom and I first moved to Pittsburgh, it took me some time to understand the character of our house in ways that led me to enhance our environment. That said, I never believed we would stay there—I did not want to live permanently in Pittsburgh—so I kept my imagination in check. At the same time, the confluence of creativity, talent, and resources needed to develop and realize my vision did not converge until we returned to Philadelphia.

Tom understood my desire, but he also wanted something else out of our move from Pittsburgh. For the first time in his life, he wanted our physical surroundings to reflect his professional success. He expressed this wish only once, perhaps recognizing that it was out of character, and because of that I remember.

My husband possesses a quiet confidence that never veers toward arrogance. At client entertainment events in Pittsburgh, guests would sometimes assume that whoever introduced Tom was his superior, when, in fact, he was the most senior executive present. He let the misconception stand, understanding that status mattered more to others than to him. I was often tempted to find a tactful way to correct the record, but I never did, recognizing that the impulse came from my own need for clarity rather than Tom's for recognition.

We began our nine-month renovation of the Paoli property in January 2012, while we still lived in Pittsburgh. I traveled regularly to the Philadelphia area to meet with the contractors and the design team. On one of my return trips to Pittsburgh, I phoned my mother, unaware it would be the last time we would speak. I made the call from the Sideling Hill Service Plaza on the Pennsylvania Turnpike. Late morning, and the sparkling light by which I had started the journey had given way to clouds. I remember thinking I would not miss the dreariness typical of

Pittsburgh winters. The Starbucks coffee warmed my hand. I looked at the few cars in the parking lot and felt an odd kinship with my fellow travelers, none of us home.

I wanted to say more than *Happy Birthday*, but my mother sounded exhausted. She told me she wasn't having a good day, so I kept my message brief. I resolved to call her back the next day, but by then she was in the hospital and soon thereafter in hospice.

In the weeks after my mother died, thoughts of her filled my journal. I struggled to describe the absence of someone with whom I had remained at a distance. It felt as if there had been some kind of atmospheric change, some quality in the air itself that was no longer present. I had not realized how much hope I'd nurtured for our relationship until I had to abandon that hope.

My grief went beyond longing for my mother. I grieved for what I had never possessed—a mother to whom I could feel attached in ways that allowed me to embody that sense of emotional and physical well-being. Her love was something I understood intellectually but could not internalize in the deeper sense of myself that does not rely on language.

When memories of her threatened to overwhelm me, I kept sorrow on the periphery by looking elsewhere—to our Paoli property and the decisions and tasks associated with its transformation.

Our renovations began with the bones of the house. We raised floors to make them uniform throughout and lowered the ceiling in the living room. We removed walls in some places and added them in others, eliminated useless doors—changes intended to center the house and create a natural flow to the way we moved within it. Mindful of the generous and abundant windows, we privileged the views outside. When you entered the foyer, your gaze was drawn to the wall of windows at the far end of the living room. From there, grasses and meadow were visible, and beyond them a stand of holly trees we planted. During our first year, we stopped mowing the grass in large sections of the property to create a meadow that inspired the birds to nest.

Our home's elegance revealed itself quietly in the well-crafted furniture, handmade rugs, refined lighting, in the colors and textures chosen to link one space to another. In contrast to the anonymity of my childhood home, paintings and ceramics dressed the walls. Photographs of our terriers, Gilbert and Annie, of other family members, of Tom and me at different ages could be found in most rooms, often sharing space with books.

I wanted each room to hold your gaze by offering something of beauty. It could be the view to the garden, or a single graceful chair that invited you to linger. In the living room, an upholstered divan stood parallel to and close to the windows. In winter, especially, I sat there sometimes in early morning's lavender light. Other mornings, I chose the deep armchair and ottoman under one of the kitchen's skylights. The movement of clouds and sun dappled the pages of the book in my hand.

Until I started to think more deeply about the ways in which my childhood home told a story about my family, and especially my mother, I had not recognized how our failure to care for Pine Street continued the theme of displacement, begun for my mother during the war. We lived there without investment, as if at war with place. We never risked attachment.

Our home in Paoli influenced Tom and me in different ways and over time. It helped him navigate his retirement from PNC, the financial services company for which he worked for thirty years. The house and grounds offered proof of his achievements, something that could endure after his professional legacy was no longer his to shape and preserve. Once he retired, he continued to improve the property by focusing on an engagement with the external landscape, much as I did with the interiors. We installed a fence around ten of our eleven acres to keep a herd of twenty deer from destroying the new trees and shrubs we planted, leaving the last acre accessible to them. Tom created a path that wound under trees and through the meadow, so that we could wander.

Overseeing our house's renovations and furnishings distracted me from grief, but it was more complicated than that. In the aftermath of my mother's death I lived between worlds, one physical and the other emotional. Leaving our house in Pittsburgh was made easier because I could look forward to inhabiting another. And I was making the journey between being a daughter whose mother was alive in the world to one whose mother was dead. Creating our home allowed me to bear an ending.

At my mother's celebration of life party, I read my comments, as did Billy, while Lydia and Henry allowed inspiration to carry them. I could not have spoken without my script, prepared as if for a performance. At the same time, my words felt intimate, addressed not only to the audience but to my mother. And also, perhaps, to myself, as a reminder.

How fitting, and predictable, I think now. That I would once more give my words to my mother, as she gave me her stories. Language both a bridge and a barrier.

I could hear her voice in my head when I began reading.

"Never chew gum," she admonished. "It will make you look like a cow." I chew gum only when I am alone in the car.

"Don't put your hands in your pockets. It will ruin the line of the suit." I leave the pockets sewn shut in fine clothing.

"Never shave your legs. You will have to do it all the time." I managed a small rebellion by ignoring this advice.

"Stand up straight." I do my best.

My mother imparted other, more complex lessons. She did so through the stories she told and also in the ways she extended herself to the many young people who frequented Pine Street. They found in her comfort and guidance not available to them elsewhere.

I spoke about a gift I'd given my mother when I was a teenager. She referred to it as her talisman. When she moved from Philadelphia to Texas, she wrapped the clay figure in tissue and carried it in her purse. After she died, I took the little creature. Small enough to fit in the palm of my hand, he's mostly a long snout and round head, his forehead wrinkled in concern. My mother told me that she treasured him because he looked like he loved humanity. Though she would not have admitted it, I think she aspired to do the same. Despite being keenly aware of human weakness, she still allowed for the existence of nobility in character and deed.

She used to say that I should "reach for the stars," that everyone should, because if you do not, you remain "forever in the mud." She was speaking about courage and the willingness to put my faith in the future. My mother tried to do that, and against odds I never faced.

And finally, I told the audience that my mother had urged me to honor the good intentions of others. She encouraged me to appreciate efforts at friendship and love, if made sincerely, even if the results fell far short of my expectations and hopes. I realize now that she might have been asking me to include her in that same recognition.

Others contributed remembrances that day, but it's Billy's childhood friend John I remember. John, my brother's roommate at Pine Street during the years they both attended Penn, a time when it seemed that my mother and our family home reflected a mutual undoing. John, now a middle-aged man, but in whom I recognized the kind boy who had once tried to tell me that I deserved happiness.

I had raised concerns about his attendance, even though I had not wanted to exclude him. "Mom loved John," Billy insisted. But my brother still had to talk to his friend about his alcohol abuse, warning him that his drinking could not make him one of our concerns that day.

John approached the podium, sheets he had torn from his sketchbook in his hand. A gifted sculptor, whose once golden persona had dimmed. He looked haggard, and his hands holding the dense sheets of paper betrayed a slight tremor. I thought of the effort required to walk those steps to the podium, knowing of our doubt.

I saved the pages John composed and from which he read that day. He referred to my mother as a "Lady—capital *L*," who had drawn to her "a surprising and potentially unruly cast of characters" over whom she presided, displaying such "patience, equanimity, and acceptance." He remembered the lavish meals my mother sometimes cooked, with leftovers lasting in the fridge for several days, depending on who visited Pine Street. I recall my mother's meatloaf, the size of a sofa cushion. She never tried to feed specific individuals, it seemed to me, just anyone who happened to be hungry.

Remembering a long-ago Christmas Eve, John offered an anecdote to illustrate the love and devotion my mother inspired. While visiting his parents in the suburbs, John learned that we did not have a Christmas tree. Though it was already early evening, he set out to do something about it. With the help of two friends, also members of Pine Street's cast of characters, he identified a suitable candidate in an abandoned nursery slated for redevelopment. Without any thought of logistics, other than borrowing a car, the three friends chopped down the tall cedar and then transported it to our house in West Philadelphia via the expressway, one of their band crouched in the car's open trunk to hold the untethered tree in place during the forty-minute drive.

I do not remember the cedar, delivered late Christmas Eve, but I retain an image of its stand-in. Lydia, in a doomed attempt at holiday cheer, had hung glass balls on the potted palm that stood in a corner of Pine Street's living room. I suppose it is telling that I can recall that lonely palm rather than the gift.

I achieved what I had hoped for by honoring my mother. I was able to offer some last words of love and gratitude, if not to her directly, then in the presence of others, which gave them substance. The emails and letters that arrived after everyone had returned safely to their own homes confirmed that my welcome was as warm as I had intended. The celebration *a great success*, I'd like to tell my mother. Perhaps she knows.

None of this suggests that I have become the matriarch of my family. That position remains vacant. Sometimes Tom and I talk about hosting family reunions with my siblings and their families, though I admit to liking the idea more than what I assume would be the reality. I continue to be more at ease with solitude than sociability, more protective than generous when it comes to sharing our home. When I invite someone to enjoy our domestic space, I am bringing them into my life, into intimacy. And it is there, still, where I sometimes hesitate.

In *Trauma and Recovery*, Judith Herman argues that recovery, which requires ongoing effort and is never complete, occurs in three stages, with central tasks associated with each stage: the establishment of safety, remembrance and mourning, and reconnection with ordinary life. My mother and grandmother both endured complex traumas, though I know far more about my mother's experience. Neither woman had access to the resources or expertise that would have helped them recover. They each survived, but at a psychological cost.

Though my mother never worked through those three stages, I believe she tried. I see her stories of the war and her much later disclosure of her rape at sixteen as efforts at remembrance. But she could not allow herself to grieve in a conscious way. And her avoidance of pain exacted a price: a deadening of feeling.

I *had* her history, my mother said of me. She meant possession of the photographs, documents, and recorded interviews—evidence of her past. But her assertion suggests a deeper meaning beyond ownership. *To have* also means "to suffer from" and "to be subject to the experience of another." I was born to a deeply wounded mother, and her wounding passed on to me with greater power than it did to my sister and brothers, because I was her first child and also a daughter.

But to reduce my mother to her injuries, to think of her only as damaged, would be both simplistic and unfair. And yet, those injuries were determinative in the way she parented me.

Without realizing it, my mother gave me the most protected and deepest part of herself—her buried trauma. I became the embodiment of what she herself could not tolerate. She could never, no matter how strong her desire, embrace me.

A mother sets the tone of her relationship with her child, and ours was one of discord. Later, when I might have changed our narrative by being more responsive to her efforts to reach me, I did not. I accept responsibility, even blame, for that. But a pattern to the ways in which I responded to my mother had already been ingrained.

In his memoir, *Memories, Dreams, Reflections*, Carl Jung wrote that he believed himself to be under the influence of things or questions left incomplete and unanswered by his parents, grandparents, and more distant ancestors. It seemed to him that he had to address questions that fate had posed to his forebears, or as if he had to complete, or perhaps continue, things left unfinished.

My mother remained a prisoner of her traumatic past. Through the stories she shared with me, I learned the contours of that prison, and unlike my mother, I can be free. She walled off parts of herself to survive, but that meant she remained fragmented and unable to fully inhabit her own life.

Going forward, my responsibility is to continue and complete what she could not. To make myself whole. To heal.

Tom and I lived in our Paoli house for eight years before selling it to another family. In the end, our renovations led us to restore parts of the house that had deteriorated as a result of the prior owner's neglect, problems not evident at first. The same held true for the surrounding land, where, under our stewardship, the trees languishing from lack of care had a chance to recover. Tom and I saved the place, if not from ruin, then a slow decline.

With that property, I had the freedom and resources to achieve my vision for the haven I sought. I had wanted to create a place of calm and loveliness. I succeeded. And in so doing, I satisfied something of the yearning engendered at Pine Street and could finally separate myself from that place and time.

We departed Paoli to settle in a smaller and less demanding house closer to Philadelphia, but still in the verdant suburbs. The move increased our freedom to travel, with France being our preferred destination, a geography that speaks to us both. In our new home, I benefit from something learned in our former one—an appreciation of the richness and potential of the language of physical space, as well as that vocabulary's limitations.

I had believed our Paoli property would be our forever home. But nothing is forever. Except love and grief, and the way they are intertwined.

Works Consulted

de Botton, Alain. *The Architecture of Happiness*. Pantheon Books, 2006.

Forsyth, Frederick. *The Odessa File*. New American Library, 2012.

Friday, Nancy. *My Mother/My Self: The Daughter's Search for Identity*. Delta, 1977.

Fromm, Gerard M., ed. *Lost in Transmission: Studies of Trauma Across Generations*. Karnac Books, 2012.

Herman, Judith. *Trauma and Recovery: The Aftermath of Violence—from Domestic Abuse to Political Terror*. Basic Books, 1992.

Judt, Tony. *Postwar: A History of Europe Since 1945*. The Penguin Press, 2005.

Jung, C.G. *Memories, Dreams, Reflections*. Edited by Aniela Jaffé. Translated by Richard and Clara Winston. Vintage Books, 1989.

Keyes, Frances Parkinson. *Came a Cavalier*. Julian Messner, 1947.

Rogers, Annie G. *The Unsayable: The Hidden Language of Trauma*. Ballantine Books, 2007.

van der Kolk, Bessel. *The Body Keeps the Score: Brain, Mind, and Body in the Healing of Trauma*. Viking, 2014.

Wolynn, Mark. *It Didn't Start with You: How Inherited Family Trauma Shapes Who We Are and How to End the Cycle*. Penguin Books, 2017.

Acknowledgments

I would like to thank Brooke Warner and her team at She Writes Press for believing in this memoir and guiding it to publication. I also extend my gratitude to the editors of journals in which earlier versions of two of these essays appeared, one under a different title: "In Black and White" in *Water~Stone Review* and "Powers of Attraction" in *Under the Gum Tree*.

My writing, and this memoir in particular, came to life in workshops I attended over several years at the Postgraduate Writers' Conference at Vermont College of Fine Arts. I wish to thank Ellen Lesser, the conference director, for bringing together an inspiring and generous group of writers year after year.

The seeds for this memoir were sown in a workshop with Sue William Silverman. She suggested that the dense essay I had brought forward contained multiple essays. Sue believed in this book before I did. I benefited from her wisdom and guidance in developing the first drafts of much of this material. Thank you, Sue, for always seeing potential rather than limitation. I also want to extend my deep appreciation to Lee Martin. Thank you, Lee, for your encouragement and your advice, and especially for helping me identify the moment toward which I was writing.

Thank you, Janna Marlies Maron, for thoughtful and timely developmental editing and for creating More to the Story, a community of women writers of nonfiction. And thank you, Ken Harvey, for reading and commenting on the manuscript multiple times and at different stages of development. Your counsel was unfailingly wise and consistently kind.

I wish to thank Dr. Alan Molitor, a gifted psychologist, and, in my view, a poet at heart. Alan, your support and wisdom have, over many years, helped me to understand and accept that without shadow, there is no light.

I am grateful to friends who also happen to be gifted writers. Thank you, Barbara Caver, for sharing the journey to write and publish a first memoir. I wish to thank the five writers who belong to what my husband, Tom, calls my community of faith: Jean-Marie Saporito, Jan Elman Stout, Anne Shaughnessy, Jolene McIlwain, and Dave Barnette. I know you are there to cheer me on and to remind me to believe in myself. I hope you know that I believe in each of you. And to Jolene, in particular, thank you for your insightful feedback whenever I requested it, and for your generosity in all ways.

I have been lucky in my friends, some of whom are part of my chosen family, and also in the family into which I was born. I want to thank my brother Billy for reading this memoir while it was still in development and for sharing his recollections of our parents and life in our family home. His memories deepened and clarified my own. I also wish to recognize and thank my sister, Lydia, and my brother Henry for trusting me to tell stories about our shared childhood. You could have tried to silence me, especially when my story crossed over into your own, and you never did.

And finally, to my husband, Tom: You are my partner, my person, my love. This memoir would not have been possible without your support. Thank you for your consistent encouragement and for inviting me to recognize that the glass is at least half full.

About the Author

Margaret Whitford served in leadership positions within the nonprofit world for twenty years, including ten years in the social justice field, before turning to writing. Her work has been nominated for the Pushcart Prize and appears in *Water~Stone Review*, *Brevity*, *Under the Gum Tree*, and other publications. A dedicated Francophile, she and her husband divide their time between Concord, Massachusetts, and a small village in Provence.

Learn more about Margaret and *The History We Carry* at www.margaretwhitford.com.

Author photo © Andre Toro Photography

Looking for your next great read?

We can help!

Visit www.shewritespress.com/next-read or scan the QR code below for a list of our recommended titles.

She Writes Press is an award-winning independent publishing company founded to serve women writers everywhere.